The Experimental Knowledge of Christ

and additional sermons
of John Elias (1774-1841)

The Experimental Knowledge of Christ

and additional sermons
of John Elias (1774-1841)

Joel R. Beeke, editor
Owen Milton, translator
Iain H. Murray, biographical introduction

REFORMATION HERITAGE BOOKS
Grand Rapids, Michigan

REFORMATION HERITAGE BOOKS
2965 Leonard St., NE
Grand Rapids, MI 49525
616-977-0599 / Fax 616-285-3246
e-mail: orders@heritagebooks.org
website: www.heritagebooks.org

10 digit ISBN #1-892777-77-0
13 digit ISBN #978-1-892777-77-5

Cover: Painting of John Elias preaching at the Calvinistic
Methodist Association in Wales, reproduced with the permission
of Lylfrgell Genedlaethol Cymru / The National Library of Wales.

For additional Reformed literature, both new and used,
request a free book list from Reformation Heritage Books at the above address.

John Elias had an overwhelming conviction of the truth and efficacy of the Gospel as a means of salvation, and of the inerrancy of Scripture. There was an intense seriousness in his preaching, and never a suggestion of humor. His voice was haunting and powerful; his finger stretched in accusation or raised in warning brought mockers to their knees. In theology he was an unreserved Calvinist and opposed with great determination the tendency to flirt with "Modern Calvinism," still less with Arminianism. After the death of Thomas Jones he was the unchallenged leader of the Calvinistic Methodists. He was a man of indomitable will and unyielding principle, and this produced a kind of autocracy which many younger men—and some of his contemporaries—resented. In political matters, too, he was a bitter critic of the radicalism that was emerging among Welsh nonconformists. He was a constitutionalist of the old school, with a decided bias in favor of Toryism. On the other hand, he was energetic in his promotion of moral virtue and social betterment. This, however, did not prevent his being nicknamed "the Anglesey Pope" because of his hostility to democratic agitation and Catholic emancipation. Even so, his influence as a preacher far exceeded that of any of his contemporaries, and the legend of his miraculous eloquence in the cause of the Gospel has not died away even yet in Wales.

— Dr. Tudor Jones

Foreword

Great sermons of past generations by great preachers who have been signally used of God should always be in demand. Believers should read them with the relish of a person digging for hid treasure, all the while praying for God to once again use such sermons to foster genuine revival.

This book contains eleven great sermons by the great Welsh itinerant preacher, John Elias (1774-1841), all newly and ably translated from the Welsh by Owen Milton. Here you will find a feast of biblical, doctrinal, experiential, and practical food that shows how great preachers in ages past proclaimed the whole counsel of God over a period of time while remaining faithful in expounding individual texts in accord with their major themes. These sermons, which richly expound nearly every major doctrine of grace, are as relevant and helpful as when they were first written. Here you will find the sovereignty of God and the responsibility of man persuasively expounded. Such themes as God's sovereign calling of sinners, the experiential knowledge and fullness of Christ, the dangers of ignoring the gospel call, earnest prayer for the Spirit, the greatness of God's peace, the believer's love for Christ, the blessing of a contrite spirit, and the immanency of the Second Advent are set forth with convicting power. Practical themes such as how to listen to preaching and how to respect governmental authority are also expounded with fresh clarity. Elias's sermons exhibit all the strengths of a godly preacher-pastor-writer. Read them slowly and prayerfully, and, with the Spirit's blessing, you will grow in the grace and knowledge of Jesus Christ.

Our hearty thanks is extended to Iain Murray for allowing us to preface the sermons with his illuminating article on Elias's remarkable life and ministry, first printed in *The Banner of Truth*, no. 5 (1957), pages 5-14. For a fuller biographical treatment of Elias, buy and read Edward Morgan's *John Elias: Life, Letters and Essays* (Edinburgh: Banner of Truth Trust, 2004). May God graciously raise up such spiritual giants and grant such spiritual preaching again in our day of small things.

— Joel R. Beeke

Table of Contents

BIOGRAPHICAL INTRODUCTION

John Elias 1774-1841

Iain H. Murray

There have been men who made the most profound impression on their own generation, yet whose very names are well-nigh forgotten by posterity. Man "fleeth as a shadow and continueth not," and another generation takes his place on the stage of life. Such is the shortness of life that few find time to obey that scriptural command—"Inquire, I pray thee, of the former age.... Shall not they teach thee, and tell thee?" (Job 8:8-10). As a result, those glorious works that God wrought among their forefathers are unknown, and the lessons they ought to have learned from them wholly lost. One cannot consider the life of John Elias without being sadly persuaded that such observations are true. Though he died less than two centuries ago; though his preaching was attended by such evidences of divine power as have not often been seen in the British Isles, promoting a great awakening in North Wales; though his influence as a minister of Christ in his own day was second to none—the fact is that his life is now neither known nor remembered by the vast majority.

John Elias was born near Pwllheli, Carnarvonshire, Wales, on March 6, 1774. His parents were not religious, but under the hand of his godly grandfather he was brought to fear God at a tender age. By the age of seven he had read through the Bible from Genesis to the middle of Jeremiah. Soon after, when his aged grandfather was unable to walk with his grandson on Sabbath days to hear the preaching of the Methodists, the young boy would continue to walk without a guide or friend upwards of ten miles to hear the Word of God. His distress at his parents' failure to observe God's commands caused him to weep much, and at length prevailed upon them to hold family worship. Though between the age of fourteen and sixteen (Elias tells us) he experienced great inward conflict—"there was a strong inclination to become light and trifling like my contemporaries"—these serious impressions did not leave him, and the concerns of his soul remained the one thing needful in his mind. From his earliest days he had heard stories of the great work of God in South Wales and of the revivals that had occurred under the preaching of Howell Harris and Daniel Rowlands. The former Elias could never hear for he had died in 1773, but Rowlands, in his old age, was still preaching with great power at Llangeitho. As soon as he felt strong enough for the walk of eighty miles, Elias was determined to journey south to Llangeitho. But one Sabbath morning, in his seventeenth year, on going to church in Pwllheli he was overwhelmed with the mournful tidings of Mr. Rowlands' death. Little did Elias realize at this time that he himself was to be in the north what Rowlands had been in the south!

North Wales at this time was a scene of spiritual darkness. The Established Church was dead, and the people were given over to all manner of ungodliness. When Harris had preached in the north in 1741, he had very nearly lost his life. But there were some in the north who had been converted under Rowlands or Harris and who began to form Methodist societies as in the south. Their leader was Thomas Charles, who settled at Bala in 1783. God's time to favor them was about to come. In 1791, a great awakening occurred at Bala. Charles, writing in that year, says, "We have had a very great, powerful, and glorious outpouring of the Spirit on the people in general. Scores of the wildest and most inconsiderate of young people of both sexes, have been awakened. Their convictions have been very clear and powerful...divine truths have their own infinite weight and importance on the minds of the people...at one time there were but very few who had not felt awful impressions on their minds, producing foreboding fears respecting their future existence in another world." The following year, Elias, now eighteen, joined a large company of young people who were to attend the Association meeting at Bala. (These Associations were regular meetings among the Welsh Methodists, when believers gathered to be addressed by several ministers.) As they walked to Bala, a distance of forty miles, Elias says their time was filled with praise or discourse concerning the Bible or sermons: "They were indeed most anxious for the unspeakable favor of meeting with God. When we came there we observed crowds from different places, meeting together, and the whole multitude, appearing as persons of one mind, and engaged in the same important business.... God owned the preaching in an extraordinary manner, making his servants like a flame of fire. The saving operations of the Spirit were most clear and powerful on the people; and the divine glory rested on them.... I had such delight and pleasure in the fellowship of these godly people that I could not live separate from them. I determined to join them."

It was about this time that Elias was brought to a state of peace in his own soul, and he began to be burdened for the work of the ministry. In 1793, Thomas Charles wrote, "A very general awakening now prevails through the greatest part of the county of Caernarvon." At Christmas 1794, the monthly presbytery meeting in Carnarvonshire received John Elias a preacher. "Brethren," said an old minister, "when I am in the dust this young lad will be a great man." Never was the ministry undertaken with more gravity and solemnity. Apart from one or two Puritan works he had read few books, but, says Morgan, his biographer, "he was so well acquainted with the chief subjects in every chapter in the Bible from the beginning to the end, that he could easily make use of them on any occasion." On Elias's first appearance as a minister at an Association meeting, he opened in prayer, the effect of which was, says one who was present, that "all around me were in tears as well as myself; indeed we trembled as if we were going to appear before the judgment seat of Christ." It made a deeper impression than all the sermons they were to hear at that Association. After he had preached a few times, the rumor traveled the country that a great servant of God had been raised. At one church, where he was sent to preach in the place of another, because of his youthful appearance the members felt doubtful at first whether they would allow him to preach, "but before the sermon was over he appeared unto them as a seraph come from heaven."

Elias's ministry was of an itinerant nature, and even after 1799, when he married and settled at Llanfechell in Anglesey, he continued to visit all parts of the land, awakening a dead and sleeping people. The effects that resulted from his preaching are truly indescribable. Though many might come to hear him only out of idle curiosity, "in the twinkling of an eye their souls and spirits were absorbed with greater things. Trifles vanished; great realities appeared; God became great, as well as Jesus Christ and His precious blood; and they left the meeting in an agonizing struggle for their own salvation."

At Denbigh, in 1800, when many assembled in the open air to hear Elias, such a real dread of punishment and hell fire fell upon the people that many screamed in despair. In 1802, Elias visited Rhuddlan, one of the strongholds of Satan, where thousands attended Sunday fairs—scenes of riot, revelry, and all manner of evil. On one such Sunday afternoon, Elias and a party of believers took up their stand outside the New Inn. The sound of fiddling and dancing from the taverns was loud in their ears, and there were some hundreds of pleasure-bent people before him. Elias gave out Psalm 24 to be sung, then prayed in such a manner that awe and dread took possession of the dense throng. The din of the fair was gone when he read his text, Exodus 34:21: "Six days thou shalt work, but on the seventh day thou shalt rest; in earing time and in harvest thou shalt rest." After expounding the verse, he showed from Scripture how God visited Sabbath-breakers with punishment. He answered any excuse which might arise in their minds. Then he cried to the people with all his might, with his arm lifted up and tears flowing down his face: "Oh robbers, oh robbers, oh thieves! Alas! Stealing the day of the Lord! What! Robbing my Lord of His day! Oh robbers, the most vile and abominable." These words shook the people like the shock of an earthquake; they were filled with fear, and many said after the sermon was over that they would not for the world go there again. It put a complete end to these fairs.

Rarely has the power of the world to come been so present in a man's preaching as it was in that of Elias. People listened to him "as men that were going to the Judgment Day." He would at times suddenly say, "Stop! Silence! What are they saying in heaven on the subject?" Or he would exclaim, "Stop! Silence! What do they say in hell on this awful subject? Consider the shortness of time, and the approach of eternity. Everything will be over with us here below very soon, and we shall be in an eternal world before long."

No ministers of the gospel in Wales at this time doubted that "the fear of the Lord is the beginning of wisdom," and they lived under the impression that "it is a fearful thing to fall into the hands of the living God." The famous incident of Michael Roberts at Llanidloes in 1819 demonstrates the effects which followed this manner of preaching by others besides Elias. Roberts, on arriving at this place the evening before he was due to preach, was deeply stirred in his spirit by beholding the evident marks of ungodliness in the speech and actions of the inhabitants. "After going into his house for the night," reports Owen Jones, "he could eat nothing; during the whole of the night he slept none at all, but wrestled with God in prayer; nor could he take anything to eat the following morning. The service was to be at ten o'clock before the Red Lion Hotel. As it was an Association, there were a great many people present from all parts of Montgomeryshire. His text was Psalm 1:5, 'Therefore the ungodly shall not stand in the judgment.' He described the judgment with such vividness that a great solemnity came over the whole multitude. He described the ungodly losing the trial, and unable to 'stand.' He described them as overwhelmed with extreme despair, the pallor of death on their faces, and their knees trembling. The preacher turned to the judge, and said: 'O, mighty Jesus! Withhold Thine hand; say not a word more unto them; they are already in the agony of death; they are already overwhelmed.' The reply was: 'No; I have one word yet more to say to them; and that word I must say to them; after that—not another for ever! And this is it: *Depart from me, ye cursed, into everlasting fire!'*... Some hundreds of ungodly men were immediately cast into the condition of the jailer of Philippi after the earthquake.... Some had forgotten altogether where they stood, some swooned and fell down, some wept, many were stricken with the paralysis of guilt, and others seized with the pangs of despair. After Michael Roberts had finished, Ebenezer Morris, one of the greatest preachers of his day, was unable to fix the attention of the people; he finished after a few minutes, and the service was closed."

But although they considered that the greatness, purity, and justice of God in punishing sin was to come first in preaching the gospel, they were equally instrumental in declaring the all sufficiency and excellence of Christ in an overwhelming manner to needy sinners. More was accomplished by single sermons than is accomplished in years of preaching today! Once Elias was called to preach at Pwllheli where the state of religion was known to be very low and discouraging. "A great spiritual darkness and lethargy had prevailed there for upwards of ten years," writes Morgan. "Elias was greatly moved, when he rose up to preach, and took those words for his text, 'Let God arise, let his enemies be scattered' (Psa. 78:1). The truths delivered by him then, had, under God's blessing, the most happy and astonishing effect; many of the people fell down to the ground in great terror, crying for mercy. It is said that no less than 2,500 persons were added to the church in Carnarvonshire that year, in consequence of the powerful impetus which was given by that extraordinary sermon."

It was in Anglesey itself that the effects of Elias's preaching were most visible. "Awful indeed was the state of things there, and evil beyond expression," writes Morgan. Drunkenness, fighting, smuggling, and adultery were prevalent. The societies of believers were few and small. Within a short time the whole island was transformed, these sins became uncommon; smuggling was done away with; those who had plundered wrecked vessels took their booty back to the sea shore; horse racing and play acting were given up; owners of windmills stopped them on the Sabbath day; and, within forty years, forty-four chapels were built and filled with congregations.

Very high views of church membership were held in these times, and Elias tells us that such questions as the following were to be put to professed converts. "(1) Have I been brought to see and consider the greatness and infinite purity of God, before whom I am, at all times? (2) Have I seen that I am a responsible creature, bound to give an account of my thoughts, words, and actions? (3) Have I believed that I fell awfully in Adam? Have I seen myself an enemy of God, and that I deserve the wrath of God to all eternity on its account? (4) Have I discovered the value of Christ as a Saviour to lost sinners? Is He precious to my soul, and is He in my estimation altogether lovely? (5) Does my soul desire to know Him more, and to love Him better, to enjoy more of His fellowship, and to be more conformable to His image?"

Four children were born into the humble home of Elias, but only two survived infancy. Elias's wife kept a shop in the village to provide for them all until her death in 1829. When it was necessary for the children to be away from home at school, the kind of loving counsel they received from their parents illustrates the spirit that reigned in the homes of believers in those days. Elias writes thus to his son: "Avoid more carefully the things that injure thy soul: abhor those things as the most bloody murderers, yea the murderers of thy soul: thou knowest what they are; levity and jesting, hastiness and passion.... Think of the great God, who is everywhere present with thee, and seeth thee at all times—think of thy soul, which is immortal, and to endure everlastingly—think of the shortness of thy time, it is but little; when a day has passed, there is no possibility of recalling it in order to be spent again. Think frequently of death; of the judgment day; of eternity, we shall soon be there! Think of Jesus dying, and be amazed and happy." "My dear daughter," he writes in another letter, "spend not the time of thy youth in vanity and sin; thou must ere long give an account to God of every day and every hour of thy life, and for every word and action! Do not allow thyself to live in any known sin, nor in the neglect of any known duty. O! do not neglect secret prayer, but go to the throne of grace as you are, and humbly commend thyself to God through the Mediator Jesus Christ—implore His mercy to pardon you, His Spirit to direct you, His providence to protect you." Both children grew up to adorn the gospel.

It is not possible here to give a chronological account of Elias's life, but surely enough has been said to cause us seriously to attend to the following questions. Wherein lay the power of this man's ministry? Why has such power departed from us today? What was there in his life and doctrine which led to the great usefulness of his preaching? Where is the contrast between him and us most evident? In an understanding of such questions lies the only hope for the visible church today. We can answer them by looking at Elias first in terms of his private life, in reference to his doctrine.

Elias obtained his strength and authority from very close communion with God. "Satan is not afraid of the soldiers," he writes to a fellow minister, "though they are armed—of the knowledge or gifts of any preacher; but he is afraid of the presence of God, the leader of the true army. As the Philistines cried out, 'Woe to us, God is come to the camp.' So a cry would be made in hell, and a great alarm in the regiment of Satan, if God should be pleased to appear among you." Elias was well acquainted with "appearances" in his own home. His daughter said of him, "To live in his family was to a great degree heaven upon earth. I can never forget the light that followed our family worship. And never can I forget the tears I saw on the chair in his study by which he bent on his knees; though nothing was heard, we were well aware that he was pouring out a profusion of tears in his secret prayers. Many times did I observe him coming out from his chamber, like Moses coming down from the mountain, with so much of the image of God upon his countenance that no one could look him in the face."

Sentences like the following recur throughout his letters, and illustrate what was uppermost in his heart: "The ministers of the Gospel are under great necessity of being experimentally acquainted with the work of the Holy Ghost.... Oh, that we might have more of the communion and fellowship of the Holy Ghost!" "O, may each carefully observe that nothing separates or darkens between his soul and God. Cherish a tender conscience, and a broken heart, avoid an indifferent spirit, a hard heart, and a sleepy conscience. Press on for more intimate fellowship with God in private.... O, brethren, be not easy without His presence. I often fear that many are now in the churches that know no difference between the hiding and the shining of His countenance. O, be not satisfied with anything instead of Him. Let us cry earnestly that we may be continually made more heavenly; we shall be here but a short time." "The greatest loss I feel, is that of the Spirit, and earnestness of secret prayer." "If private prayers were more frequent and earnest, the public ministry would be more effectual." There is room to give only one instance of the remarkable answers which attended Elias's prayers. Once at Carnarvon, he found some mountebanks were corrupting the place with their sinful amusements. On their refusing to desist, Elias in a chapel meeting prayed to the Lord to put a stop to their proceedings. "Many," says Morgan, "were struck with the fervency, and power of his prayer, as being extraordinary. The next day, awful to relate, three of the players came to an untimely death; the wagon in which they traveled was overturned, and they were killed! Two others, in the act of dancing on the rope, fell and broke their necks!"

"Elias's character," writes Morgan, "was composed of determination, perseverance, and mental energy, to a high degree.... The character of pious gravity was stamped on all he did. He reflected Christ's image upon the world. He was never known to have cast off the livery of his noble calling upon any occasion. The seriousness of his appearance would repel any disposition in others to levity and frivolity." Owen Jones truly comments, "The strength of his character as a preacher *lay in the hold which the great truths of the Gospel had taken upon his own spirit.*" This was in no small measure due to the high value Elias placed upon study. He never allowed his constant preaching and long itinerant journeys to lessen his deep conviction of the relationship between hard study and powerful preaching. Although he never had any regular schooling, he not only mastered the English language (having been brought up to speak only Welsh), but studied sufficient Greek and Hebrew to be able to consult the original Scriptures. Such writers as John Owen and Jonathan Edwards were his constant textbooks; in his letters we find him recommending such Puritans as Brooks and Flavel. Dr. Jenkyn said of Elias "that he had collected more of the Puritan

theology into his mind than any man of his age." Reflecting on his
early ministry Elias wrote, "I was enabled to persevere day and night
at my studies without fatigue and delay. I am now even in my 67th
year, learning; and see greater need of knowledge daily." Again he
writes, "It is not in an easy, careless manner, that we get learning,
understanding, and knowledge; no, it must be by labor, industry, and
toil (Prov. 2:3-4)." "Those who knew him best," says Morgan, "testified that his sermons cost him many a tear, many an earnest
prayer, yea many a sleepless night! His chief delight was in his study,
and he would even bring his Bible down with him to his meals."

In the latter years of Elias's life, there was a noticeable with-
drawal of the powerful operations of the Spirit from the land in
general. Writing in 1837, he says, "The light, power, and authority,
formerly experienced under the preaching of the word, are not
known in these days! The ministry neither alarms, terrifies, nor dis-
turbs the thousands of ungodly persons who sit under it.... No
experimental, thoughtful Christian can deny but that God has withdrawn Himself from us, as to the particular operations of His
Spirit, and its special manifestations of His sovereign grace." The
explanation Elias gives of this declension illustrates his doctrinal
position, and his consciousness that the preservation of the favor of
God depended upon their maintenance of the Word in its purity.
He believed that nothing so ruined churches or dishonored God as
erroneous teaching: "It is an awful thing to misrepresent God and
His mind in His holy word!" "The Lord," he wrote, "hath favored
us, poor Methodists, with the glorious truths of the gospel in their
perfection. Alas! Errors surround us, and Satan, changing himself
into an angel of light, sets these pernicious evils before us, as great
truths!" These evils, as the following quotation from his diary
shows, were the appearance of Arminian errors in Wales in the
nineteenth century. "The connexion" (that is, the church, which
arose in Wales in the eighteenth century awakening) "was not
called Calvinistic Methodists at first, as there was not a body of the
Arminian Methodists in the country. *But when the Wesleyans came
amongst us, it was necessary to add the word Calvinistic, to show the dif-*

ference. There were, before this, union and concord, in the great
things of the gospel, among the different denominations of Christians in Wales. The Independents agreed fully with the Methodists
in the doctrines of grace. They used to acknowledge the Westminster Catechism, as containing the substance of their doctrine.... All
from the least to the greatest, preached very clearly and plainly. The
chief subjects of their discourses were these: the fall and total corruption of man; his miserable state under the curse, and the just
indignation of God; his total inability to deliver and save himself;
free salvation, by the sovereign grace and love of God...." It was a
departure from these truths that caused his deep concern. "The
great depth of the fall, and the total depravity of man, and his awful
misery, are not exhibited in many sermons in scriptural language;
it is not plainly declared that all the human race are by nature, 'the
children of wrath'—that none can save himself—that no one
deserves to be rescued, and that none will come to Christ to have
life. There are but few ministers that fully show that salvation
springs entirely out of the sovereign grace of God."

The Arminian teaching was that Christ has purchased redemption for all, but that the effectual *application* of that redemption is
limited and determined by the will of man. To Elias such teaching
involved a denial of the completeness of Christ's work and offices;
it led to an underestimation of the effects of the fall on man, and
therefore to correspondingly low views of the necessity of the
Spirit's almighty work in conversion. "I do not know," he writes,
"how those that deny the total corruption of the human nature, and
that salvation as to its plan, its performance, its application, is of
grace only, can be considered as faithful ministers.... *Unsound and
slight thoughts of the work of the Holy Spirit are entertained by many in
these days, and He is grieved thereby.* Is there not a want of perceiving
the corruption, obstinacy, and spiritual deadness of man, and the
consequent necessity of the Almighty Spirit to enlighten and overcome him? He opens the eyes of the blind; subduing the
disobedient, making them willing in the day of His power; yea, He
even raises up the spiritually dead! It is entirely the work of the

Holy Ghost to apply to us the free and gracious salvation, planned by the Father in eternity, and executed by the Son in time. Nothing of ours is wanted to complete it.... *Man, under the fall, is as incapable to apply salvation to himself, as to plan and to accomplish it."*

No one saw the dangers that threatened the visible church from these errors more clearly than Elias. Towards the end of his life he writes, "It is a dark night on the church, the depth of winter, when she is sleepy and ready to die. It is still more awful, if while they are asleep they should think themselves awake, and imagine that they see the sun at midnight!... The watchmen are not very alert and observant. The multitude of enemies that surround the castle walls, bear deceitful colours; not many of the watchmen know them! They are for opening the gates to many a hostile regiment! Oh let it never be said of the Welsh Calvinistic Methodists, 'Their watchmen are blind.'" He knew of no remedy for such a situation save a restoration of the truth in its purity. "If people are anxious for the favor of God's presence, as the early fathers in the connection were blessed with, *let them take care that they be of the same principles*, under the guidance of the same Spirit.... When the Spirit is more fully poured on people, those precious pillars of truth will be raised up out of their dusty holes; then the things of God shall be spoken in 'words taught by the Holy Ghost,' and the corrupt reasonings of men will be silenced by the strong light of divine truth. May the Lord restore a pure lip to the ministers, and may the old paths be sought, where the road is good, and may we walk in it; there is no danger there."

John Elias died on June 8, 1841. Some 10,000 people attended his funeral at Llanfaes in Anglesey, a multitude of solemn feelings possessing their hearts. "Ah," writes Morgan, "the thought of seeing him no more till the last day! The day he frequently and seriously dwelt upon in his discourses, with power almost inspired. Oh Mona! Oh Wales! Oh ye multitudes of men, how will it be with you, when you will next see that most eminent minister?" "Remember them," commands the Apostle, "who have spoken unto you the word of God: whose faith follow, considering the end of their conversation. Jesus Christ the same yesterday and to-day, and for ever" (Heb. 13:7-8).

The Danger of Losing One's Soul While Seeking to Gain the World

"For what is a man profited, if he shall gain the whole world, and lose his own soul? Or what shall a man give in exchange for his soul?"
—Matthew 16:26

It is very sad to think that such a reasonable creature as man behaves so unreasonably and unwisely in relation to spiritual and eternal matters. Men generally lose the best while pursuing the worst, and by going after the least things, they leave the greatest behind.

That part of man that we call his soul is the most important part; it is that which chiefly distinguishes between him and the animals. Man's superiority over the irrational creature lies in his soul. Man does not excel the animal in terms of the substance of his body—both are made of dust—nor is there much difference in the form of his body; soon the appearance of the man will be as wretched as that of the animal, in the grave. The soul is what makes the man. Even so, he is of little value, in spite of his superiority. The soul can live without the body, as it shortly will. Before long, we shall be living in another world, in a form very strange to us now: naked souls without bodies. The soul can live without the body, but the body cannot live without the soul.

The words of the text are taken from a conversation beginning in verse 24, "Then said Jesus unto his disciples, If any man will come after me"—that is as a disciple or follower of Me—"let him deny himself"—abandon and forsake his ways, his wisdom, and his own righteousness, "and take up his *cross*"—that is, let him suffer quietly the tribulations and crosses that he will encounter by following Me, and be My disciple. Let him take up the cross and not be discouraged or sink under it. Let him take it up on his shoulder, and should he be afraid of failing, let him strive, and let him pray to Me, and I will strengthen him.

The next verse speaks of the danger of denying Christ, by denying the profession of Christ in the face of trial or persecution on account of the religion of Christ; Christ shows that no one gains anything by denying Him. "For whosoever will save his life (that is by denying Him), shall lose it." It is as if Christ were saying, when tribulation or persecution come because of the Word, the man who denies Me rather than die as a martyr will die eternally. Whoever tries to save his life will lose it forever. And on the other hand, "whoever will lose his life for my sake shall find it"—that is, the man who lays down his life as a faithful martyr for the sake of the Son of Man shall find it a second time. It will be restored to him in the resurrection, and he will not suffer the effects of the second death.

The greatest of fools are they who abandon what is most precious in order to gain what is most worthless. The text is brought in as a reason to show the foolishness of saving the body, or gaining worldly profit, only to lose the soul and eternal life. "For what is a man profited, if he shall gain the whole world, and lose his own soul? Or what shall a man give in exchange for his soul?" (Matt. 16:26).

There are three points to be noted concerning these words:
I.   That men by nature want to gain the world, even the whole world
II. That by gaining the world, they lose their souls
III. That the market is poor and the exchange foolish: "What shall it profit..."

I. Men by nature want to gain the world, even the whole world

Men try to fill the emptiness left in the soul through the loss of God, and they do this by seeking to satisfy themselves with the things of the world. In this context, we understand the "world" to be everything visible, or all the desirable things of earth, as it has already been described in the divine revelation. Let me direct you to 1 John 2:15-17. According to John, by the "world" we are to understand chiefly "the things that are in the world." These are comprised under three names: the lust of the flesh, the lust of the eyes, and the pride of life.

To "win" these things means to desire them, to crave them, to cherish them, to love them immoderately, and to choose them as a portion and an inheritance. It means to find our supreme pleasure in them, and to ask for happiness in this world where it is not to be found. These are the words referred to in the verses: "Love not the world, neither the things that are in the world. If any man love the world, the love of the Father is not in him. For all that is in the world, the lust of the flesh, and the lust of the eyes, and the pride of life, is not of the Father, but is of the world" (1 John 2:15-16). Because the natural man cannot supply the lack of God in his soul, he attempts to make up for it with the things of the world.

1. *The lust of the flesh.* Lust is one of the things that are in the world. There is no substance in lust—it is vanity, a shadow without substance. Lust reaches for and strives after happiness but never attains it. The lust of the flesh refers to the animal lusts, such as adultery, wantonness, drunkenness, and gluttony. The lust of the flesh is that which requires the flesh to satisfy it, and demands the loan of a body to fulfill it. Through these lusts, thousands of men lose their souls.

2. *The lust of the eyes.* This refers to desire for the things that the eyes see, such as houses and lands, animals, produce of the earth, silver and gold, and all the treasures of this world together with its splendor. To lust after them is to be greedy for them, to love them inordinately, to choose them instead of God, and to love them more than God. It is to take them for a portion and inheritance, and to seek our delight and pleasure in them. Through this lust, again, thousands lose their souls.

3. *The pride of life.* Here is the yearning for the honor of this world, the longing that men should have the best opinion of them and think highly of them, and that important people should have great respect for them. It is to be swollen with pride, self, and arrogance.

Some boast of their beauty, others of their dress, some of their gifts, and others of their riches. That is the pride of life. Once more, in their mad pursuit of these and other vanities, thousands of people lose their souls.

Men by nature seek to gain the world, the whole world, and for all this fail to find satisfaction. There is no satisfying lust. Feeding lust only inflames it. Those who gorge themselves on the lusts of the flesh—adultery, drunkenness, and carousal—no matter how they are filled, only add drunkenness to thirst, and create a craving for more. The more a man strives to fulfill any lust, the greater will his desire be for it. Salt water only makes a man thirstier, and feeding a sinful lust only excites it. "He that loveth silver shall not be satisfied with silver" (Eccl. 5:10). The more he has of anything, the more his love for it will grow. The man who loves honor will not be satisfied with honor. Should his honor increase like that of Haman, he will not be one step nearer to satisfaction; on the contrary, his lust will multiply as though he would have all the honor of the world for his own. There is enough evidence, but little understanding of this. Men, by nature, seek to gain the world.

II. Men, by gaining the world, lose their souls

This does not mean the loss of the existence of the soul. That would be gain for the ungodly. Rather, it is the happiness of the soul that will be lost. The soul will never lose its existence, although it will lose its happiness; but it will exist forever in one of two conditions. Many in the world do not believe this, as we saw lately in the case of the traitor who was hanged on the scaffold in London. On the edge of eternity, he cried with all the boldness of the flesh, "Now for the grand secret!" He meant by this, "Now to see whether there is a soul or not, or even another world in which to lose the soul!" That poor wretch has seen the truth now. Although the soul has been lost, it will continue in existence forever. It is not the loss of existence that is meant, but the loss of eternal blessedness, peace, and comfort for the soul.

Although man has lost his soul through sin, God has devised

a way to save it, and to ignore this is to lose the soul. By gaining the world, men lose their souls—they let the day of grace go by while they involve themselves with things that will pass away. In one sense, this is how everyone loses his soul. Trying to gain the world along one of the various paths mentioned is the broad way to hell and destruction. The attractiveness of sin and the lust of the flesh are like tempting bait on the hook, which men greedily swallow. So the soul is lost.

Gaining the world is the reason the soul is lost, by preventing men from seeking and searching for that which keeps the soul. We have a notable example of this in the parable of the rich man. This man was enjoying all the bliss this life had to offer. Feeding the flesh was his concern. The lust of the flesh was his rule of life, and according to his lust, he ate, drank, and clothed himself. The world and its lust was his object, his rule and his all, until he drowned in it to destruction. In the end, the soul went to hell. If you follow the lust of the flesh, you are facing the same danger.

We have another example of men destroying their souls by following the lust of the eyes, in the parable of the great supper. This lust prevented two of those who excused themselves. When they were invited by the servants of the king, they both excused themselves. One excused himself saying, "I have bought a piece of ground, and I must needs go and see it: I pray thee have me excused" (Luke 14:18). The other said, "And another said, I have bought five yoke of oxen, and I go to prove them: I pray thee have me excused" (v. 19). How many are going, one to his field, another to his business, while neglecting their souls!

Again, in the twelfth chapter of Luke we have an example of the second kind of lust: the lust of the eyes. Here is a man whose land produced a good crop. He was governed by the lust of the eyes. His affections and his heart were set on things that are seen, and he was so foolish as to present all his goods that he had harvested to his soul. But God said to him, "Thou fool, this night thy soul shall be required of thee: then whose shall those things be, which thou hast provided?" (Luke 12:20). He gained a great part of the world, but he lost his soul.

Others want to gain the honor of the world. This is the pride of life: despising the precious soul for the sake of the esteem of a few men. It is sad to see men craving after foolishness and taking pains for sheer vanity, pursuing the regard of men and refusing the gospel, seeking the glory of men and despising the command of God, and in this way, losing their souls. Oh, proud man, if you are here, listen for the sake of your soul! The proud is the man the Lord "knoweth afar off." To gain the world like this is your only trouble—you are likely by gaining the world to lose your soul, and to gain the world and lose the soul is the worst bargain imaginable. By running after the world, men lose the only opportunity to keep their souls.

III. The market is poor, and the exchange of gaining the world and losing the soul is a foolish one

"What shall it profit a man?" It is a poor exchange on many accounts. First, it is a poor exchange because you must die and leave the world, and therefore lose it after you have gained it. When you lose the soul, you actually lose the world as well.

Second, benefits of the world are not to be compared with the benefits of the soul. The world will end, but the soul will continue. The world is only earth and will be soon burnt, but the soul lasts forever. It is impossible to relate the depth of the poverty, misery, and distress of him who loses his soul eternally. Are not the greatest pleasure, honor, and profit to be found by seeking the world? The answer is that if it were so, what would it profit you if you lose your soul? You will lose more than you gain. Therefore, consider the matter, look at it from all sides, like Moses, and make a wise choice. Do the same as the merchants when they settle their accounts. They put the profit on one page and the loss on the other, and if the loss is more than the profit then they give up the business. Do the same for yourselves. Oh, soul, soul! The world is a poor exchange for the soul, if you had it. The soul is worth infinitely more than the world!

I draw attention to three additional doctrinal matters arising from these words.

1. That man has a soul
2. That the soul is in danger of being lost
3. That we are in a position today where it is possible for the soul to be saved, and it is dangerous to allow this opportunity to pass

1. *That man has a soul.* "But there is a spirit in man: and the inspiration of the Almighty giveth them understanding" (Job 32:8). Every man has a soul, and God is the giver of that soul. The fact that you have a soul fits you for the work of discerning spiritual matters, and enables you to fly across the boundaries of time to consider what there was before time existed—and what there will be when the world is burned, and time will exist no more. It is because of this that you are able to entertain ideas and thoughts of the invisible world. If you had no spirit, you could not think about the spirit. It is only the soul that can think about the soul. Without the soul, and that which is invisible, you would be unable to grasp things that are invisible. I am certain that man has a soul, but what it is I do not know entirely. I cannot describe it. But although we cannot comprehend what it is, there is abundant evidence of its existence. Close your eyes to all the impulses of the body and you will be aware of a mind that understands, that reasons, and that shoots here and there without any assistance from the body. Yes, you will one day be a spirit without a body. And after leaving the body, the conscience will be more alert, the will stronger, the affections more fervent, and all the faculties of the soul healthier and more complete than they ever were in this life. This great crowd will before long be naked spirits without bodies. The bodies will be gathered to a little space in the earth, and the spirits flying to some place in the distant world, either to everlasting and unspeakable misery or bliss. What a serious matter! I can speak only to the ear, but I am glad to think that there is One who can speak to the conscience. Many seek honor and glory for the body without considering the value of the soul. If I did not believe that you had a soul, I would not labor to preach, publish, or make known the method of salvation. But

because you most certainly have a soul, I am sad to lose you, and am most anxious to have you saved. I am ready to spend and be spent if I can be the means of saving someone.

2. *The soul is in danger of being lost.* You have lost the image of God on your souls already, as well as your right to happiness. You are again in danger of being lost, while under the preaching of the gospel and the possibility of salvation. There is a danger of losing the soul, and to lose this is the most dreadful loss of all; it is an infinite loss. To lose health, senses, relatives and the various comforts of this world are great losses, but the greatest loss is that of the soul. Oh sinners, careless, indifferent, unconcerned about salvation, many of your companions in sin have now lost their salvation! Therefore, while there is still hope, grasp the opportunity to save your souls.

3. *There is a way to keep the soul today, and we are in the situation where it is possible to keep the soul. It is dangerous to let this time pass.* One of His tasks as Shepherd is to seek the lost, and one of the chief purposes of His coming into the world was to seek and to save that which was lost. His soul was much burdened for the salvation of the soul, to have you who believe reconciled to God, released from the hold of the devil, and from the clutches of unbelief, to deliver souls from the wrath of God, and the judgment to come.

Now is the time for keeping, but it is dangerous to let this time go by. The time to save a soul is short. That time is now, and today is the market day for our souls, but I fear that there are some who are alive today who will have no more opportunity for salvation. It is offered today, "How shall we escape, if we neglect so great salvation?" (Heb. 2:3). Whoever is lost, I have pleasure to declare in your hearing, and with authority, that an exchange of the soul is to be had today by all who hear me. God is today on His throne, offering His mercy for the sake of the atonement and the sacrifice that was made on the cross. He forgives sins, delivers from the power of Satan, releases from the curse of the law, justifies the ungodly, and saves to everlasting life.

Therefore, sinner, come as you are, throw yourself on the Savior, fall at His feet, and say, "Oh God, save my soul, through the sacrifice of the Mediator, and wash me in His blood! Although I have been very foolish until now, because there is hope for me and still some of my day of grace left, I cry from the depth of my heart. Oh Lord, in the way Thou hast ordained, save my soul!"

How serious it is to look at this gathering and to realize that each one has a soul of greater value than the world, though many of them do not know it! I turn from you towards Him who is able to save. "Oh God, have mercy on this congregation! Put Thy fear in them, cause them to see their danger, and show them where they are going, and what kind of a world they will be in before long. Let none go home today unsaved. May beneficial effects follow the Word, to save and to turn men to Christ. Have mercy, and save souls, or men will lose their souls and their bodies. Cause great concern to fall on the inhabitants of the entire world for the salvation of their souls." Amen.

The Experimental Knowledge of Christ

"That I may know him, and the power of his resurrection, and the fellowship of his sufferings, being made conformable unto his death." —Philippians 3:10

No people have ever enjoyed greater advantages than we have in the matter of gaining a historical, fundamental, and experimental knowledge of Christ. As far as means are concerned, there is nothing more for God to do for us. He might well ask of us as that which was asked of Israel, "What could have been done more to my vineyard, that I have not done in it?" (Isa. 5:4). We have great privileges and abundant calm and freedom to enjoy them. Indeed, it seems to me we could hardly expect more. And yet, there is reason to complain of how little even of the factual knowledge of Christ many people have, and how little basic and elementary knowledge many hearers possess. There are many, according to their privileges, who ought to be instructors, but who still need to be taught the first principles of the things of God. An ignorance of Christ beyond imagination commonly persists among hearers. Men are neither prepared to seek for Christ nor to talk about Him. If occasionally He does enter their conversation, it is more often as the God of nature and providence than as the God of salvation. Many are happier to consider His commonplace and natural mercies than His covenant relationship with sinners in Christ, as if to say they want nothing to do with Him in that respect. If they were asked about the person of Christ, His work and offices, the manner in which He executes His offices, His grace, His mercy, the sufficiency of His atonement, His glorious intercession in heaven, and His coming at the end of the world in judgment, we would generally find utter ignorance.

Again, there is great scarcity of experimental knowledge of Christ. Knowledge of Him through the revelation of the Spirit is hardly to be found anywhere and is rarer than any other branch of knowledge. There are many who have a considerable amount of factual and historical knowledge of Him, but who have practically none of this experimental knowledge. My text contains a description of this invaluable knowledge, an experimental knowledge, a revealed knowledge, an effectual knowledge of Christ.

In the preceding verses, the apostle gives an excellent description of true religion. He shows first the kind of religion he had formerly practiced, and then the great change that he underwent through grace. His views, opinions, experience, and life were changed; the things which once were gain to him, he counted loss for the sake of Christ. "But what things were gain to me"—the things I prized, the things that were my very life, the things that were heaven to me—those very things, I say, "I counted loss for Christ." I count them loss, I consider them, and I judge them, having weighed the matter carefully. This is not something imaginary or superficial for me but serious, sure, and authentic. It is not a conclusion I arrived at hastily. I have examined it, weighed it, scrutinized it, and tested it to the limit, over a long period of religious profession. And the opinion I formed then, I hold now, after twenty-nine years of professing Christ, and preaching Him, and suffering for His name's sake: "I count all things but loss for the excellency of the knowledge of Christ Jesus my Lord" (Phil. 3:8).

The knowledge of Christ is superior to every other knowledge. We could have every other knowledge and still have nothing, for there is no other knowledge that is able to save a sinner. If we had the knowledge of all the philosophers and astronomers, and understood all mysteries, and yet had not the knowledge of the crucified Christ, our souls would have no benefit whatsoever.

The knowledge of Christ excels all other knowledge, for it alone satisfies and brings contentment to the soul. This is the knowledge that fills the greatest vessels, and is sufficient for the broadest and strongest of faculties. It was enough for men like Sir

Isaac Newton, men of immense attainments and immeasurable comprehension. Although they searched heaven and earth, they did not find satisfaction. Although they penetrated the treasures of the oceans and the worlds of space, they failed to fill their vessels. Although they possessed the ability to leap from world to world in the vast universe, in pursuit of that which would satisfy their brilliant intellects, they failed to discover what would bring them complete contentment. But there is in the experimental knowledge of Christ, more than enough to fill all the vessels of men and of angels—"which things the angels desire to look into" (1 Peter 1:12). No doubt the angels studied minutely the prophecies about Christ before He came in the flesh. They especially took notice of Him when He came in the flesh to live on earth. They gazed on Him in astonishment when He was a baby in the manger, they watched Him closely as He made His troubled way on earth, they watched Him in the wilderness, being tempted by the devil (when they were sent to minister to Him), and they watched Him in His struggle in the garden as He cried, "If it be possible let this cup pass from me" (Matt. 26:39). They watched Him in His sufferings under the scourging on the cross. We do not know, however, if they were allowed to see more, or whether the veil was drawn between them and Him in the time when the storm was at its worst. And even now they desire to look into these things, yes, even today. Sometimes they are down with the saints, ministering to them who are the heirs of salvation; sometimes they are before the throne, seeing and hearing more and more. Day after day, they are learning new things in the Bible, and learning much also in the sermons and the society meetings as they hear godly men speaking about Christ. Then they are in heaven, looking at the face of the Man Himself on the throne, without a veil. The knowledge of Christ keeps them fully occupied, and their vessels full to overflowing.

This knowledge also saves a sinner and brings the greatest benefit to the soul, which is something no other knowledge does. For all I know, Paul knew Christ better than any man, and yet he says here, "that I may know him," as if he accounted himself as knowing nothing because of his yearning to know more. In spite of all he knew of Him, he wanted to know more. Indeed, the greater our knowledge of Christ, the greater our thirst for more. Those who know most about Him are the ones who long to know more about Him, and be more conformed to Him.

I have three things on my mind to say to you arising out of the text:
  I.   That men by nature are without Christ
  II. That Christ is to be had
  III. That the greatest gain on earth is to have Him, even though this should mean the loss of everything

I. Man by nature is without Christ

The man who is without Christ is the poorest man in the world, and the most pitiable on earth. He who is without Christ is without forgiveness of sins. He has not been released from the power of Satan; he has not been removed from the reach of the wrath of God, and he has no right to life on the other side. To be without Christ is the greatest poverty possible—and yet this is the condition of man by nature.

II. Christ is to be had

There is a welcome today for all who will come. Preaching Him is our task; publishing this is the work of the ministers of the covenant, and great is their honor. Here is a message worth declaring to a company like this, and a testimony worthy of a hearing by a multitude: "Christ is to be had." He is to be had by all kinds of people this side of the grave. Christ is to be had by the guilty, the lost, the poor, and that freely, without money and without cost.

III. Gaining Christ is the greatest gain, though everything else be lost

If a man gains the world and loses Christ, he would make a very bad bargain—indeed, he would be an everlasting loser. But the man who loses the world and gains Christ makes the best bargain ever, and will be an everlasting winner, because to have the world is nothing but deception and disappointment. To gain Christ is an infinite mercy.

Of course, by gaining Christ, there are some who lose many desirable things. However, they receive far more in exchange. Many refuse Christ and religion, preferring the pleasures of sin, and loving the present world. Even so, there are some who through infinite mercy are given a heart to receive Christ. One of the most outstanding examples of these was Paul. For the sake of Christ, he lost his reputation and his temporary comforts. Instead, he endured cold and nakedness, faced danger in many forms, and at last, suffered martyrdom. For all this, in God's estimation, the greatest gain was his. Whatever he lost, he received sufficient in its place. To have Christ is to have enough. Having Christ is enough to answer all our needs, to make up for all our losses, and to make us happy forever. Out of these considerations Paul cried, "and be found in him," and "I do count them but dung, that I may win Christ" (Phil. 3:8).

There are two things to be understood in receiving Christ. One is that we are seen as being in Him for our justification. The other is to know Him for our sanctification. Here is righteousness sufficient for the sinner in every circumstance: sufficient in the face of death and all the wanderings of the wilderness and sufficient for the scrutiny of a stern judgment. This is a righteousness which will profit for all eternity. Let us all cry to have Christ, to know Him, and to be safe in Him—"and be found in him." Those in Christ are in a secure ark, safe from the fiery flood, with nothing to fear from the storm that will soon break, because in Him they are acceptable to God, with a right to eternal life. They are in a safe refuge, secure from the wrath of the avenger, and safe from every vengeance. In Christ the weakest and the poorest may find shelter, live in every storm, and escape when the end comes.

"That I may know him." There is something remarkable about this statement. Paul knew Christ already; he knew Him better than anyone, and yet his chief concern was that he might have a greater and deeper knowledge of Christ. Despite the knowledge he already possessed, he had a thirst for more knowledge. People who think they have enough knowledge of Him are very different in their affections and experiences from Paul. Paul longed to experience the

virtue of Christ for his sanctification, and therefore dealt much with Him, and yearned passionately for His fellowship on earth.

I notice further two doctrinal matters arising out of the text:

1. That an experimental knowledge of Christ is essential to true religion
2. This knowledge brings the soul into fellowship with and conformity to Christ

1. An experimental knowledge of Christ is the sum and substance of true religion. Religion will never save anyone unless he has an experimental knowledge of Christ. Many make much of some kind of religion that will be of no use on the other side. Only that religion with an experience of Christ in it will avail there. This is the only religion worth possessing; it is the only religion profitable for living or for dying. The experience of the love of God in Christ will cause us to forget our anxieties and uphold us in death and in the judgment to come. My people, seek that religion which has the experimental knowledge of Christ in it.

You ask, "What is an experimental knowledge of Christ?" To have an experimental knowledge of something means to try it, to possess it, and to enjoy it ourselves. You must not merely read or hear about it; experimental knowledge is far more than that. You may read many a sweet chapter about Christ, and no doubt you have heard many a faithful sermon about Him, and yet, you may be without a saving knowledge of Christ. But an experimental knowledge of Him is to prove, see, and feel what you have read and heard about Him. "That which was from the beginning, which we have heard, which we have seen with our eyes, which we have looked upon, and our hands have handled, of the Word of life" (1 John 1:1). An experimental knowledge of Christ is an absolute necessity for true religion, and to prove Him in this way is the sum of religion. In order to explain this further, I emphasize three points which I consider of the utmost importance for everyone to understand.

i. The gospel bears witness to Christ
ii. Faith is necessary to receive this witness

iii. It is the soul that truly believes, proves, feels, and
knows beyond any question that Christ truly embodies
that which has been testified concerning Him

Take this as an illustration. Imagine a renowned doctor coming to the house of an ill friend of yours. Upon seeing him, the doctor says, "There is only one thing that can cure an illness like this, and I am the only one who has this cure." That is historical knowledge, knowledge of the facts. Your friend now knows the facts about his illness, the doctor, and the only cure. The man then thinks about these things, and seriously considers them in relation to his own case. He feels the sickness at work in him exactly as it was described, and recognizes the signs and symptoms mentioned by the doctor. So accurate is the description that the man is compelled to believe that the doctor has made a perfect diagnosis and has said nothing but the truth. If it is in fact the truth, then he is a dying man apart from the cure. The fear of death grips him, and he trembles as a result of that fear. In his distress, he remembers the doctor's words about the infallible cure, and he determines that he must have it whatever the cost. He sends for the doctor, he receives and takes the medicine and follows scrupulously the instructions on the prescription. The result is that he is cured. His sickness leaves him, his fever recedes, the pain in his head eases, his stomach functions again along with all the indications of recovery. After a while, he is perfectly well. This is the experimental knowledge of the doctor. Spiritually, the same is true with regard to Christ.

Experimental knowledge is not something weak and ineffective, but potent and powerful, with great results as a consequence. Whatever Christ is called in the Bible, and in whatever character He is portrayed and offered to sinners to receive Him as such is experimental knowledge. Let us, for example, take Christ as the way, according to His own description of Himself as the way to the Father. How is He the way? When a sinner is convicted, he sees that he is far from God, and that the way he is walking is very dangerous. He tries every way he can devise, but all he meets is the frown and the wrath of God. He realizes that the way to the tree of life is guarded by the cherubs with the flaming sword, and that he is utterly without hope of coming to God in peace. In his extremity, he remembers Christ and the way that was opened through His sacrifice, His atonement, His blood—a lawful and legitimate way for the sinner to come to the Father. Then he makes no further attempt to approach God by any other way, but only by leaning on Christ as the true way. Through Christ, he is received by the Father. That is experimental knowledge of this truth.

Here is another example. It is a common saying, and one which you have heard many times: the blood of Christ gives peace to the conscience. But still, there are many who have not understood what is meant by this. The sinner who is pricked and convicted by the Holy Ghost—this sinner knows the plague of his own heart and feels his inner corruption; his conscience troubles him unbearably and tells him that a terrible storm is approaching so that it is hell with his soul; he remembers that the blood of Christ can purify the conscience. When this man runs for his life to Christ, and gives himself up to Him, Sinai is silenced, the conscience is pacified, and a perfect calm descends on his troubled breast because he has found deliverance in the merit of his Surety. This is peace of conscience by the blood of Christ.

Once more you have heard that Christ satisfies all the desires of the sinner. Anyone who knows Christ in this way will cry out with the Psalmist, "Whom have I in heaven but thee? And there is none upon earth that I desire beside thee" (Ps. 73:25). The soul that has seen the loveliness of Christ, and has had a sight of His beauty, has seen Him in all His glory as the Savior of poor sinners, so that he is ready to cry out with ecstasy like the church in the Song of Solomon, "As the apple tree among the trees of the wood, so is my beloved among the sons. I sat down under his shadow with great delight" (Song of Sol. 2:3).

You have also heard of His love and His grace, upholding in every distress, and giving shelter in the greatest storms. But there are some here who have been in the fire, and He preserved them there so that the fire did not hurt them, and the form of the fourth walked in their midst. Others have been on Sinai, and found in His sacrifice a way to still the troubled elements, the fiery mountain and the thunder. These are able to testify to His love and grace because they have proved Him.

The Word also says that Christ is a Physician, a Shepherd, a Leader, and everything else that a sinner needs in order to make him a complete Savior. To receive Him in such a manner is experimental knowledge. We need to know Him better in this way, and to increase in this knowledge. And if we have this knowledge, what else is required? The answer is that we must *increase* in this knowledge. Paul says to the Colossians, "As ye have therefore received Christ Jesus the Lord, so walk ye in him" (Col. 2:6).

We must also strive to learn Christ. What is meant by this? To learn Christ is to go on in the knowledge we have spoken about. None of us has learned Him so much that we have no more to learn. And it is not true knowledge unless it creates in us a thirst for more. To learn Christ is to increase, to go on in this knowledge until we have used it all. "Put ye on the Lord Jesus Christ," and when we learn Christ properly, that is what we will do. What does it mean to put on the Lord Jesus? It is to live to Him, to lean on Him, to make use of Him entirely, all that He is to the sinner. It is to put off the old man with all his deceitful lusts, and to put on the new man. Put on the Lord Jesus by denying ungodliness and fleshly lusts, and by living soberly, righteously, and godly in this present world.

Experimental knowledge of Christ is the sum and substance of true religion and conformity to Him. To raise the sinner to the image of God—and to know Christ aright—is the sum of religion. Will any religion avail that does not include experimental knowledge of Christ? Absolutely not, for we have been predestinated to be conformed to Christ. It is to the image of Christ that the Holy Spirit is forming us; He is fitting us and preparing every stone in the spiritual temple. It is in the likeness of Christ, and in His image that the saints will come out of the grave, perfectly formed and fitly joined together. The work will be completed.

It is in the knowledge of Christ and conformity to Him that

the strength, sweetness, profit, and usefulness of religion consists. Through this knowledge the image is to be received. And the sweetness, strength, and usefulness of religion will always escape you without this knowledge. We see here the incomparable virtue of the great salvation found in Christ. This salvation is such that to know it experimentally is to have all our needs supplied. Those who have this experience are able to recommend Christ to others. They can say to the weakest and most miserable of men, "We were once as wretched as you, but we met Christ—we heard, saw, and proved His love, His mercies, and His saving virtue. It is on Christ Himself that we live, and therefore we can commend Him to others, and speak well of Him."

"That I may know him." There is infinite worth in knowing Him. Knowing Him keeps men from longing after the things of earth. It causes them to mortify sin, strengthens them in temptation, and keeps them from falling in trials. It fills their souls with strong consolation, sustains them without falling until the end, and comforts them there. It upholds them in the valley of the shadow of death, and preserves them fearless in the judgment. Oh, precious knowledge: who would not want it? Let us all cry for the Spirit of God to reveal Christ, so that thousands may come to know Him. Oh, that the Spirit would come to our meetings, attending every sermon with fire from heaven, in every society and Sabbath school, so that our conversation might spring from experience, and create thirst in every soul of man to know Christ, the power of His resurrection, and the fellowship of His sufferings. Let us call much for Him, and look for Him to come into our midst.

2. Experimental knowledge of Christ brings fellowship with Christ and conformity to Him. Here we have the richness of religion; we are in a mine of fabulous wealth. To call to the fellowship of the Son of God is to grant the knowledge of Him, for this is the effect. To where does God call a sinner when He calls him from darkness to light? He calls sinners to the fellowship of His dear Son. The effectual call of God to the sinner brings him into fellowship with His Son. "Truly our fellowship (we who are called) is with the

Father, and with his Son Jesus Christ" (1 John 1:3). If you are resting on the form and name, and remaining on the circumference of
religion, fulfilling its duties and with a mere profession, and without fellowship with His Son, you are still on the plain, and have not
climbed the mountain. You are still within the reach of the fierce
and terrible storm. When the fire consumes Sodom, you have nothing to expect but destruction, because your country will burn when
the fire burns Sodom. Therefore, people, run before the storm.
Your state must be changed before the flood of fire comes. Make
sure of the knowledge of Christ, and of fellowship with Him.

Finally, a word or two about the conclusion of the text: "the power
of his resurrection, and the fellowship of his sufferings, being made
conformable unto his death."

1. *"The power of his resurrection."* Oh, merciful and gracious God, as
we speak and listen to these matters, may we prove the power of
His resurrection! There is an indissoluble link between knowing
Him—the power of His resurrection—and the fellowship of His
sufferings. There is a close relationship between knowing Him and
our justification, our sanctification, the hope of glory, and our glorious rising from the grave on that great day. There is infinite power
in His resurrection, and there are marvelous results that follow.
Through His resurrection, His saints are justified, and their resurrection assured. He arose for our justification. He secured our
resurrection from the grave of sin in the new birth, and the resurrection of our bodies from the gates of death on the morning of the
great resurrection. All will be delivered from the chains of corruption through the resurrection of Christ the head. Immense might
and power were displayed in the resurrection of our Surety from
the grave, and so it will be in the resurrection of the sinner from the
grave of sin, because of "the exceeding greatness of his power." It
is the exceeding greatness of the power of the Son of God that
raises the dead to life. Nothing else can do it. And after he has been
raised by God's power, he is given grace to put off the grave-clothes,
to break the shackles of darkness, and to be released from the bonds

of death. Oh, to experience the virtue of his resurrection that raises us from the graves of our sins! May we all be brought to know Him, to prove the power of His resurrection, to live godly in Christ Jesus, and to walk to the glory of God. Knowing the power of His resurrection would raise sinners from their spiritual graves, a great and glorious company, to worship the Lamb on Mount Zion. And although it is not done at once, the work is going on. How is it being accomplished? Our great head in heaven is drawing His members, one by one, through the power of His intercession, from the grave of sin and corruption. By the same means He will keep us alive, in the face of the worst that the world and the flesh can do, until we go home to Him. Because He lives, He will quicken His members, and will sustain them until their corruptions are overcome; He will preserve them until His work in them is completed, and until they are carried to the world where there is no more death.

2. *"The fellowship of his sufferings."* Divines look at this expression in two ways. Some say that it means we are made willing to suffer for His sake. Others say that it means we crucify the old man with Him.

With regard to the first, we are indeed made ready to suffer for Him. We undertake to follow Him through distress, and to take the cross uncomplainingly until our journey is over. We bear the marks of the Lord Jesus, and "fill up that which is behind of the afflictions of Christ." To you it is given to believe in, live to, and suffer for the one who died for you. This expression also refers to the crucifixion of the old man with Christ. Our sins wither as we gaze at the cross. We mortify our corruptions as we meditate on His death. To look on Him who was pierced for us will pierce our corruption. This is the most effective means to mortify our old man. And the sight of His love in giving Himself for us will make us willing to die for Him and to suffer for Him, to die to the world and the flesh in our fellowship with Him.

3. *"Being made conformable unto his death."* This is the same as the last expression but casts more light on it. The fellowship was as extensive as the sufferings. "Always bearing about in the body the dying

of the Lord Jesus" (2 Cor. 4:10). Christ, as it were, dying again and again in us, as we suffer similar pain and anguish for Him and for His sake.

Before I finish, let me say a word or two to certain people here. To those who are tried and anxious, you who are distressed in your minds and whose hearts are heavy, you must cry much for the experimental knowledge of Christ. Through this knowledge, you will be comforted, and you will find joy in your tribulation.

To those who know Him: there are some who, by the amazing and infinite grace of God, have had an abundant and experimental knowledge of Christ. Their cry is, "That I may know him." The more knowledge of Christ that they have, the more they desire. They who know Him best are those who cry most to know Him better. They have such delight in His fellowship that they will not be satisfied until they are conformed to His image. They are pressing towards the resurrection of the dead, to see the King in His beauty, to see Him as He is, without a veil between them and His glory. They long to have that fellowship with Him that Moses enjoyed—face to face; they long to be like Him without any blemish on them at all. They yearn to be as pure as the saints will be in the day of resurrection.

Finally, to those here who do not know Him: dear people, it will be awful to meet Him without knowing Him. Those who do not know Him, He will thrust from Him in that day, and will condemn to everlasting separation under the intolerable burden of the solemn word, "Depart." But, thanks be to God, I have better news for you. Today, in His mercy, He holds out an offer to the worst of sinners. None will be refused; He receives whoever comes! He has an abundance to meet all our needs, and the offer that flows from His mercy is to fit us for His company, and to live with Him forever. Oh, infinite God! Have mercy on this gathering, bring sinners to know Thee, show them the glory of Thy Son, until they receive Him, see Him as altogether lovely, and the chiefest among ten thousand. Bless the preaching of Thy Son to bring many to know Him. Amen.

The Duty of Listening to the Gospel as the Voice of Christ

"This is my beloved Son, in whom I am
well pleased; hear ye him."
—Matthew 17:5

In terms of His human nature, Christ is no longer on earth; although His person is omnipresent, His humanity is not. Although Christ is able to fulfill His promise to be with His people wherever they are, His human nature is only in one place at one time. There are many today in every corner of the world debating His promise, "Where two or three are gathered together in my name, there am I in the midst of them" (Matt. 18:20). And so He is, according to His promise, although not according to His human form. In His physical form He is now in that place called "the right hand of the Majesty on high," "the right hand of the throne of God," the place in the third heaven that is called the "right hand of the Father." That which the papists assert is completely unreasonable, that men eat the body of Christ, and that His body is present at the mass. In the very nature of things, the body of Christ can be in only one place at one time, and that place now is the third heaven. "We have such an high priest, who is set on the right hand of the throne of the Majesty in the heavens" (Heb. 8:1). "By his own blood he entered in once into the holy place, having obtained eternal redemption for us" (Heb. 9:12). "But this man, after he had offered one sacrifice for sins for ever, sat down on the right hand of God" (Heb. 10:12).

After Christ had offered Himself this side of the veil, He went by His blood to the other side of the veil. When He had completed His work here as Mediator, in His state of humiliation, He went from here to His work beyond the veil. Here He was accomplishing our salvation, and there He is interceding to apply that salvation. And although His human voice is no longer heard, nor is His physical appearance visible to us, still there is a way to hear His voice, and to listen to Him even now. This is what our text is saying: "This is my beloved Son in whom I am well pleased: hear ye him."

These words came from the most excellent glory. They contain the testimony of the Father to His delight in His Son as Mediator. The cry came at the transfiguration of Christ, (a similar cry was heard at His baptism) on the Mount of Olives. He had with Him there three of His disciples—Peter, James, and John. There was such an incomprehensible brightness about His body that it caused His clothes to be as white as snow. Then two of the inhabitants of heaven appeared to them, Moses and Elijah; Elijah at least, I would think, was in the body, and perhaps Moses also had received his body again.

At the sight of these two shining visitors, the disciples were filled with more joy than their vessels could contain. Then Peter cried out, "Let us make here three tabernacles; one for thee" (meaning Jesus), as if to say, "Although we honor Moses and Elijah, Thou art more greatly honored; therefore we will raise the first tabernacle to Thee." One tabernacle was for Moses, as he was the greatest of his age, and the most useful in his generation, and the one who enjoyed the most immediate fellowship with God. Further, one tabernacle was for Elias, the zealous prophet and famous reformer, who was taken away without tasting death. An unusual joy took hold of them, because of their heavenly companions. It was as if they said, "Well, now we shall prosper. Before, everyone ridiculed both us and our Master, but now we will go through Jerusalem and all Judea accompanied by these famous men. And when they see these two great men and our Lord with this amazing brightness, everyone will believe."

But even as they were thinking these things a cloud came and hid them all from view, and to their great disappointment the two visitors were taken away. It seemed that the Lord was saying, "Because you have made more of My servants than you ought, and thought more of them than of My Son, I have removed them, and they are not to be your companions as you thought. But you will not be at a loss because of their absence. My beloved Son is with you, and He is worth more than them all. You do not need Moses and Elijah; neither does My church. My Son is a greater prophet than Moses, and a more powerful reformer than Elijah. Listen to Him."

"This is my beloved Son." This is a Son from eternity, and therefore without beginning. He was a Son before the mountains were established and before the hills were formed. He was neither a Son for the sake of the human nature He assumed nor on account of His humiliation, but He was and is essentially a Son. He was the Son even if there were no world in existence, or men to be saved or lost.

If He was the Son for these reasons, then the first person in the Trinity would not be called Father, and the Holy Spirit would not be the third. The Holy Spirit would be the Father, and the first person would be the Holy Spirit. He is the Son of the same substance as the Father and the Holy Spirit. Although we cannot understand the nature of the personality of Jehovah, we can believe that God understands Himself, and that He is as He testifies in His Word. "This is my beloved Son," says the Father, My everlasting Son, co-equal with Me, My own Son. And in the fullness of time He took on Him human nature and sacrificed Himself to make an end of sins, to make reconciliation for iniquity and to bring in everlasting righteousness for us.

"In whom I am well pleased." Heaven is pleased with Him in everything: in His demeanor and His words, in the uprightness of His walk, in the perfection of His life, in the purity of His teaching, and in His death.

"Hear ye him." Lean on Him as a priest, bow to Him as a king, and learn from Him as a prophet.

Let me make a few further observations from the text. Although Christ is now in heaven out of sight of all the inhabitants of earth, so that no eye can see Him, nor ear hear Him, yet He still speaks in a way that we can hear Him. And we have a responsibility to hear Him. I have just one matter arising from these words apart from various smaller points. It is that Christ speaks to us through His ministers, and we ought to listen to them as though He Himself spoke to us directly.

Christ has a voice, and it is His voice that is to be heard through His ministers and messengers. If my text required you to listen to the servants of Christ only as men, my sermon would be unnecessary, because of your earnest desire to listen. But here it is to Christ that you are called to listen, and to us as to Him. The truth is, however, that we have more hearers than He does. For every one of Christ's listeners I have ten, and the least popular preacher in the world has far more listeners than He does. Men take great delight in listening to us, without ever listening to Him. There are many reasons why we ought to listen to Him, and to the gospel as His voice.

I. We ought to listen to the gospel because there is an excellence, glory, majesty, and wonder in the gospel itself. The gospel is the voice of the Son of God, and we ought always to regard it as such. Great preachers do not make it better, and poor preachers do not make it worse. We should not listen to it just because of the flowing eloquence of the one, nor refuse to listen to it because of the stilted speech of the other, because there is a glory in the gospel itself. No man or angel can add anything to it. This is what Christ Himself says. "He that heareth you heareth me; and he that despiseth you despiseth me" (Luke 10:16). Paul writes to the Corinthians, "We are ambassadors for Christ, as though God did beseech you by us: we pray you in Christ's stead" (2 Cor. 5:20). Our sermons are best when we speak most like Christ, when we utter fewest of our own words and most of His, and when we speak as if God were speaking.

We cannot give any splendor to Christ's gospel through any gift we possess. Do not be so concerned as to which language God chooses to speak, nor what kind of messenger He uses, if he has the marks of godliness on him, and evangelical experiences in his soul.

A minister is not to be judged by his eloquence, nor by his lack of it. While you listen to us as to men only, it will not benefit you. Therefore listen to him. If there is nothing more than the listening to the messenger, there will be no worship of God, nor profit to our souls, even though God has many times blessed those who were not seeking Him. That, however, is the exception to the rule.

No message contains such excellence as the gospel. If all the noble speeches of the Greeks were gathered together, all the learned Old Testament commentaries of the rabbis, all the works of the divines who wrote on the Bible, it would be like holding a candle to the sun in comparison with the teaching of Christ.

The gospel contains more wonders than in the entire world. If we knew more astronomy than Newton, more about the planetary system than Herschel, it would be but like A, B, C alongside the advanced textbook of the gospel of grace.

II. Because it is such a delightful message and contains what is so fitting to our needs. There is nothing that God can do and that a sinner needs that is not to be found here. It is displayed in the unsearchable riches of Christ, to be distributed freely, without money and without price.

III. Because the gospel, and the gospel alone, is the means of salvation. Only the gospel can save the sinner, and if this cannot, nothing can. When heavy afflictions, the gnawing of the conscience, and the lightning of Sinai have left men hardened, we look to the gospel. But if the gospel leaves them in the same state, they are without hope. "There remaineth…a certain fearful looking for of judgment and fiery indignation, which shall devour the adversaries" (Heb. 10:27).

IV. Because the Lord, through His promises, has bound great blessings to faithful preaching, and conscientious listening to it. God does not require us to listen to everyone, for there are thousands in the world who are preaching blasphemy about God. God commands us to listen only to Christ and His ministers.

If you are persuaded from the minister's holiness of life, his evangelical experiences, the beauty of his character, and his zeal for the glory of God, that he is a minister of Christ, then listen to him.

Promises are given and blessings tied to such listening. "Go ye into all the world, and preach the gospel to every creature. He that believeth and is baptized shall be saved" (Mark 16:15-16). "Go ye therefore, and teach all nations, baptizing them in the name of the Father, and of the Son, and of the Holy Ghost: teaching them to observe all things whatsoever I have commanded you: and, lo, I am with you alway, even unto the end of the world" (Matt. 28:19-20). Blessed Jesus, is it such poor preachers as these that Thou dost send to all the nations? Would it not be better for Thee to send or go to Rome, and convince Caesar, and all the captains of the Roman army, so that Thou mightest have the authority of the state on Thy side? And then, must Thou go to Athens to collect all the learned scholars in the realm of the arts and the sciences, to make famous preachers? And again to Jerusalem, and to the great Sanhedrin, to convince the seventy of them in a minute, and all the rabbis, in order to teach the truth about God in heaven? Then the whole world would follow Thee. No! I will not go to Rome, or Athens, or to Caesar, or a few learned men in Jerusalem. Mighty Jesus, unless Thou dost carry all these with Thee they will be against Thee. That is true. And Thy disciples are so very weak to face them. Let that be so. But "my strength is made perfect in weakness" (2 Cor. 12:9) "That the excellency of the power may be of God" and not of men (2 Cor. 4:7). They say, "We cannot change anyone." But Jesus says, "I will be with you." You teach, I will come to open eyes and change men and make them new. Teach all nations, and preach the gospel to every creature. Teach the worst, the hardest, and the weakest. I will change them. I will take away the heart of stone, and give them a heart of flesh. It is in this way that blessings and success are tied to the faithful preaching of the gospel of grace. And those same blessings are tied to conscientious listening—"Hear, and your souls shall live." To listen is the task God has given you, and what follows is that your souls shall live. Hold fast to the means, and expect the blessing from God.

V. Because of the astonishing effects that follow the preaching of the gospel. "It is the power of God unto salvation to every one that believeth" (Rom. 1:16). "It pleased God by the foolishness of preaching to save them that believe" (1 Cor. 1:21). Here is the foolishness of God that is wiser than men. Here are the weapons that are mighty through God to the pulling down of strongholds. Here is what razes the towers of Jericho to the ground. This is the means by which the obstacle of the Red Sea is removed from the path of the Israel of God. God has done astounding things through preaching. One poor preacher in Jerusalem on a day like today* was the means of saving three thousand. And the virtues that accompany salvation are the same. If there were the same influences, there would be the same results. God's hand is not shortened; so let us plead that He will visit us.

VI. Because the message of salvation is the same as was the ministry of Christ Himself. What did He say when He was here in the days of His flesh? "Come unto me, all ye that labor and are heavy laden, and I will give you rest. Take my yoke upon you, and learn of me; for I am meek and lowly in heart: and ye shall find rest unto your souls" (Matt. 11:28-29). "In the last day, that great day of the feast, Jesus stood and cried, saying, If any man thirst, let him come unto me, and drink" (John 7:37). "Him that cometh to me I will in no wise cast out" (John 6:37). His voice is the same today in the ministry. He is calling sinners today. He does not today quench the smoking flax, nor break the bruised reed. Today He still carries the lambs in His bosom, and gently leads those that are with young. Therefore, hear Him.

VII. Because we have but a short time to listen to Him. We will never have another gospel, nor another time to hear it. This is the only gospel and the only time we will ever have to listen to it, although our existence will continue forever, even as long as God's. Sinner, if this opportunity passes, and you are not saved by the gospel, then you will never be saved. "Today, if ye will hear his voice, harden not your hearts."

VIII. Because of the enormity of the sin of not listening to Him.

Not even the sin of Sodom was as serious as this. "Whosoever shall not receive you, nor hear your words...it shall be more tolerable for the land of Sodom in the day of judgment, than for that city" (Mark 6:11).

IX. Because a terrible judgment has been pronounced upon all who refuse to listen to the gospel. "With whom was he grieved forty years? was it not with them that had sinned, whose carcasses fell in the wilderness? And to whom sware he that they should not enter into his rest, but to them that believed not? So we see that they could not enter in because of unbelief" (Heb. 3:17-19).

Now, let us hold an experience meeting for a few moments. Although there are some here who have never been in this kind of meeting, it might be well for them to be here. "What shall I do?" one may ask. "I am an enemy of God, exposed to His wrath, and I cannot save myself. What can I do?" Well, my precious soul, here are your instructions: hear Him. He is offering Himself to you. Everything the sinner needs is in Him. If you are a debtor, He is the surety. If you are unclean He has opened a fountain in His heart, and He offers it for the washing of the unclean. If you are naked, He has clothing. If you need direction in the wilderness, He is a leader. "I will bring the blind by a way that they knew not; I will lead them in paths that they have not known: I will make darkness light before them, and crooked things straight. These things will I do unto them, and not forsake them" (Isa. 42:16). "The Lord is my shepherd; I shall not want. He maketh me to lie down in green pastures: he leadeth me beside the still waters. He restoreth my soul: he leadeth me in the paths of righteousness for his name's sake" (Ps. 23:1-3).

Therefore let everyone hear Him. Listen to Him throughout the day. Listen to Him in every service. Listen to Him throughout the meeting, and pray that He will speak to your souls. May His blessing rest upon all the truths preached to that end. Amen.

*This sermon was preached on Whit Sunday, 1819.

Praying for the Spirit

"If ye then, being evil, know how to give good gifts unto your children, how much more shall your Father which is in heaven give good things to them that ask him?"
—Matthew 7:11

For a godly man, prayer is essential. It is impossible to be godly without praying. Prayer is as natural as breathing to the godly man, and it is by prayer that he is sustained and upheld. Since prayer is so important, it is necessary for us to know how to pray. As I realized this important truth, my mind was directed to this text.

I propose to give some plain and clear directions on the matter, suggestions that must be received by anyone who would know any measure of success at the throne of grace. First and foremost, we should pray for spiritual and eternal things, those things that concern the glory of God, and the profit and salvation of souls. This can be summed up briefly as praying for the Spirit. When we pray for the Spirit we are, in effect, praying for all the gifts of the Spirit, that which includes every spiritual gift. And when we receive the Spirit we receive every spiritual grace and gift with Him. Praying for the Spirit and receiving the Spirit are expressions full of significance. This is evident from a number of considerations: the Spirit is the author of every grace and spiritual gift; He is the revealer of every grace; and He is the one who performs every good work in us. In consequence of this, notice the following:

I. We ought to ask and pray for the Spirit
II. We must be importunate in prayer
III. Some general exhortations to pray for the Spirit

I. We ought to ask and pray for the Spirit

There are two reasons why we should pray for the Spirit. First, we should pray for the Spirit because of our need of Him. The second reason is the promise concerning Him—the fact that He has been promised shows that we ought to ask for Him.

1. We ought to pray for the Spirit because of our need of Him. We cannot profit from Christ nor see our need of Him without the Spirit. There are two things that are absolutely essential to our salvation: the work of Christ for us, and the work of the Spirit in us. The work of the Spirit in us is every bit as necessary as the work of Christ for us. Both are indispensable in salvation. It is as impossible for a sinner to be saved without the work of the Spirit as it is without the work of Christ. A sinner cannot be saved without receiving the Spirit any more than without the merit of Christ's sacrifice. We cannot persevere in the faith without the Spirit; we cannot live godly lives in the world apart from Him, nor fulfill one duty without His teaching. We cannot do anything pleasing to God except through the Spirit. We cannot love our brothers as we should, much less our enemies, unless we have the aid of the Spirit. We cannot obey the command of Christ to bless those who curse us, nor do good to them who hate us, nor pray for them who despitefully use us, nor discharge one responsibility to God or man apart from the special operation of the Spirit of grace. He is the author of every gift and the giver of every grace, and therefore we ought to pray for the Spirit. We ought not to think that it is a matter of indifference whether we have the Spirit or not; indeed we ought not to expect to be happy if we leave this world without the Spirit in us, which is the hope of glory. We cannot glorify God on earth, nor be ready for heaven, but by the Spirit. Unless we receive Him, and His saving work in us and on us, we are bound to be condemned for ever. The saints, after they have been made saints, can do nothing without the Spirit and His influences, but they need Him for the journey, to lead them step by step, and to defend them through the wilderness to the kingdom of heaven. But in His strength they can acquit themselves well. With the Spirit the weakest saint can overcome every enemy, escape every danger, and take up the cross and carry it; neither water nor fire will be an obstacle

to them. They will be led by the Spirit past every hindrance to glory, and they will be fitted for it.

2. We ought to pray for the Spirit because He has been promised. The promise directs us to the duty. There are very great and precious promises about Him in the Old and New Testaments. True, the great Old Testament promise is about the coming of Christ, the Messiah, but the great promise of the New Testament is about the coming of the Spirit, whose office is to glorify Christ in perfecting His work in the saints. "I will pour upon the house of David, and upon the inhabitants of Jerusalem, the spirit of grace and supplications" (Zech. 12:10). And the Lord Jesus says, "If I go not away, the Comforter will not come unto you; but if I depart, I will send him unto you" (John 16:7). It is as if Jesus says, "Although I am leaving you, as to My physical presence, I will not leave you comfortless, but I will send you the Comforter." The promise of the Father was to send the Son, and the promise of the Son was to send the Spirit. The Son promised that His Father in heaven would give the Spirit to them that asked Him. And so we have the promise of the Father and the Son to send the Spirit. I do not think it too much to say concerning this gift that God could not have promised more than the Spirit, who is one of the persons of the blessed Trinity. He is as fully a divine person as the Son. He is no less a person, because He is sent by the other persons. He is equal with the Father and the Son.

God could not promise more, nor give a greater treasure. Here is a promise that contains every promise. Everything we need is included in the promise of the Spirit. He meets all our needs—He can lighten us in our darkness, melt our hearts however hard they are, lead us through the wilderness, and make every grace effective in us: faith, hope, charity, repentance and obedience, in spite of all opposition from within and from without. He can give us everything, and do every work upon us and in us that we shall ever need. Again, the prayer for the Spirit is a prayer of faith. This is the prayer that succeeds. As children ask their father for what they need, so do God's children ask their heavenly Father, in the name of the Son, to give them the Spirit, and with the same confidence. The Spirit is to strengthen them, illuminate them, teach them, comfort them, lead them, and uphold them until they are in heaven. They are to ask for the Spirit to dwell in them. Is this not a very great request? It is. But not more than is promised; and it is inconsistent with God's glory to refuse or deny what He has promised. For this reason, we can be confident that the Spirit will be given to all who ask in faith, with an eye to the promise, and for the glory of Him who made the promise.

Furthermore, receiving the Spirit is the pledge of the inheritance, and those who receive the pledge will receive the inheritance also. God does not give the one without the other. Where He gives the pledge He grants the inheritance, but He will not give the inheritance without the pledge. It is foolish to imagine that we shall have the inheritance without ever having the pledge, or heaven without the Spirit. And it is needless to worry, if we have received the pledge, that we shall not also have the inheritance. The two are inseparably bound together. But, says someone, "What can I do? I have never received the pledge." To such I have the authority to tell you that pledge is to be had today, by anyone who seeks, and the inheritance will follow. Therefore, poor, seeking sinner, come. If you have a longing and desire for the inheritance, come to Him to ask for the pledge, and you will have them both. But if you are not praying for the Spirit, you do not know Christ, nor revere the Spirit, nor love the One who promised Him, nor believe the gospel which the Spirit reveals. If you do not pray for the Spirit, you do not yet know yourself, nor your entire inability to do anything to please God apart from Him, nor the impossibility of being saved except by Him. "But," you say, "we do respect Christ and magnify Him as the Savior of sinners, we would not do anything less." I tell you, friends, that you cannot do this without giving reverence to the Spirit of Christ. Those who love Christ are very fervent for His Spirit. The respect of men for the Mediator is according to their respect for the Word and the Spirit. The Spirit is the pledge of the eternal inheritance.

Moreover, we ought to pray for the Spirit to show us the path of life, and the way to be happy forever. Without having the Spirit in our lives, we can never attain to everlasting life because He is the One who, in accord with the eternal covenant, leads us, enlightens us, guides us to heaven, and makes us fit for it.

II. We must be importunate in prayer

We ought to pray fervently for the Spirit at all times. There are a number of things to be observed about this subject.

1. What we are to be fervent about
2. What it means to be fervent
3. Where we may learn fervor
4. The encouragement we have to be fervent in prayer

1. What should we be fervent about, and in what circumstances ought we to be fervent?

When is it fitting to be fervent? We are not to be importunate about everything. We are free to ask for everything we need, and to make all our needs known to Him. It is legitimate for us to ask for temporal mercies and deliverances, such as praying to be kept from poverty and scorn, sickness and disappointment and the like. If you need any of these, go and humbly ask your heavenly Father to give them. Or, you may ask Him, if it is according to His will, to save you from some trial. But here there is no place for importunity. Great fervor is out of place when we ask for temporal provisions.

But, when you ask for the Spirit, then you are to be in great earnest. Now it is impossible, as I see it, for you to be too zealous; indeed, the more fervor the better. The more passionate you are in asking for the Spirit, the more acceptable will you be in your Father's eyes. We ought to be fervent for the Spirit; He has been promised to those who fervently seek Him. And we ought to be persistent in seeking Him, because in Him we shall have all spiritual blessings. Above everything, we should be fervent for the Spirit.

2. What does it mean to be fervent? How can we be fervent without being presumptuous? What is holy importunity?

There is no such thing as a fervent heart for a spiritual blessing without a felt need for that blessing. Arrogant and vain gentlemen might appear in the guise of beggars, but they would have no incentive to persevere, because they would have no need. But the truly poor and needy man who feels his poverty and his need so much that he cannot live will be earnest. For this man importunity is proper; his life depends on the issue, whether his request will be granted or not.

There is in fervor an energy beyond compare. It shows itself in unremitting effort in word and deed, and all the faculties of the soul cooperate—the mind, the memory, the will, the affections, and the conscience. They all act together in perfect harmony. All the graces are involved, and fill the man's mouth with reasons, pleading the promises. All this is entailed in fervent prayer.

We have many examples of fervent prayer in the Scriptures, and we do well to mark them. Let me remind you of one or two. The Lord speaks to Jeremiah saying, "Therefore pray not thou for this people, neither lift up cry nor prayer for them, neither make intercession to me: for I will not hear thee" (Jer. 7:16).

Here we see that it would be customary to be fervent. We find Moses, too, calling out in his prayer, calling until there was unrest in heaven, if you will allow the expression, because God asks him, "Wherefore criest thou unto me?" (Ex. 14:15). God does not regard every prayer in that way. Although those who were near him did not hear the cry, there was in his prayer a cry that reached the throne of God. And again we hear David, "I cried unto him with my mouth" (Ps. 66:17). There was a great pleading in the prayer of David. And the prayer of our blessed Mediator was "with strong crying and tears" (Heb. 5:7). The account of the Canaanite woman is an example of astonishing perseverance, along with the great wisdom of her reasoning in support of her request to have the devils cast out of her daughter. "Have mercy on me, O Lord, thou Son of David; my daughter is grievously vexed with a devil" (Matt. 15:22). As well as her persistence and wisdom, she had immense patience to expect an answer to her request. She kept asking and asking and following Him, although He was a long time in answering. It seems to me that if He had not answered her, she would have continued crying to Him and following Him until he was nailed to the cross. If He had not given her what she desired, she would have persisted in crying, "Jesus, thou Son of David, have mercy on my daughter." She would not give in, and He would have no rest until she was successful in her mission. It is people like these, those who pray fervently in this manner, that God loves. They are people without equal. They will not give in, they will not yield, they will not be discouraged; rather, they persevere until they gain their end, which is eternal life. They are not deterred, although they may be called dogs, hypocrites, and backsliders. Rather, they look for grounds to plead, and to find reason even for such as they are to come to Christ for salvation. You of little faith, what do you make of this? If you prayed like the Canaanite woman, not one of your sons or daughters would ever have a devil, because you would insist that the Son of God attend to them, and you would give Him no rest. Pray for such a spirit!

Where is this sacred importunity to be learned? It is learned only in the school of Christ. He became poor to teach us, although He was infinitely rich. I say again, He who was rich became poor in order to teach mankind the art of begging. This was one of the purposes, and not the least, of His coming into the world. The intense groanings and passionate requests of the meek Jesus in the garden and His bloody sweat in Gethsemane are remarkable examples for us to follow, and a powerful argument for being fervent. This is what we learn in the school of Christ.

We are given great encouragement to be fervent. First, the Lord commands it in His word. "Produce your cause, says the Lord; bring forth your strong reasons, says the King of Jacob" (Isa. 41:21). And the Lord Jesus exhorts us by means of the illustration of the man who through his persistence persuaded his friend to give him three loaves.

Second, importunity pleases God. If this was not so, a man would not be at his most fervent when he is nearest God. The nearer a sinner is to God, the more earnest will be his prayer, as in the case of Jacob when he pleaded with God for the blessing. And again, if this attitude was not pleasing to God, the Spirit of God would not incline them to it.

Third, there is no question, in the face of all the evidence of the Word of truth, that faithful, earnest prayer must prevail before the throne of God. "When the poor and needy seek water, and there is none, and their tongue fails for thirst, I the Lord will hear them, I the God of Israel will not forsake them" (Isa. 41:17). How will God answer them? "I will open rivers in high places, and fountains in the midst of the valleys: I will make the wilderness a pool of water, and the dry land springs of water" (Isa. 41:18). Are these not amazing things? Of course they are, but it is as if the Lord were saying, "I will perform miracles and astonishing deeds, rather than that one prayer, especially a fervent prayer, should be offered in vain."

A final encouragement is given to us in the text as to why we may have such an assurance. "If you then, being evil, know how to give good gifts unto your children, how much more shall your Father which is in heaven give good things to them that ask him?" (Matt. 7:11). Here He appeals to their affections as parents and children. Our Lord was remarkable in His ability to draw near the people in His preaching, and in these words He comes to the parents by appealing to their emotions and their natural feeling toward their children. It is as if He was saying, "Now you are parents, but once you were children, and therefore you know the feelings and needs of children. You also have the affections of parents. You know the love of a child for his father, and also that the love of a father for his child is so great that he is ready to do anything for him."

Then comes the appeal: *"If ye, then, being evil."* They are imperfect and changeable at best. And yet, in spite of this great fault in their character, the love of parents to their children is universal. It would be monstrous to see a mother neglecting her child. It would be shocking to see a father refusing to give bread to his child. It is true such wickedness is possible today. I am afraid that there are scores of fathers and mothers in this populous city of Liverpool who through drunkenness and hardness of heart are neglecting and causing cruelty to their own flesh and blood. They have no more tenderness toward their children than animals, if that. They leave them in a worse state than the cruel ostrich does her young. But mercifully, gentleness is the common attitude of parents to their children. Ungodly parents give good or necessary gifts to their children—and that without them asking. How much more when they ask, and when out of weakness or need they beg for those things? And how much more than that will your heavenly Father give to them that ask Him?

"Give good gifts." If the father sometimes refuses to give his child a toy, he will not refuse to give him bread. If he denies him something to play with, he will not deny him the necessities of life. When the child cries to his father for bread, if there is bread to be had anywhere, he will demand it for him.

"How much more shall your Father which is in heaven?" Such powerful reasoning, and such strong encouragement and exhortation to continue in prayer! If you give good gifts, being evil, changeable, earthly, imperfect fathers at best, frequently poor and helpless; but Christ could say, "I am a good Father—perfect, unchangeable, almighty, all-powerful. You are often unable to do for your children what you would, but I can do all things. At best, you have so many weaknesses and imperfections, but I am a perfect Father, unfailing and changeless. The children cannot ask for anything that I cannot give them, nor indeed ask for more than I can give them. If a child comes to me sick, I will heal him, for I am a Father and a Physician. If he comes to me poor, I will make him rich. The more he asks the more he will receive, and the more ready I will be to give. I will be none the worse because he is poor: I have riches in abundance to share with him."

If a child calls on his father, there is a relationship between them and in virtue of that relationship, his cry goes to the father's heart, so that he cannot but hear his cry. It is true that the father loves to hear his voice, but he is too fond of him to leave him for long without relieving his necessity. If you are like this, what about your Father in heaven?

Child of God, take heart, your Father is saying, as it were, "Ask of Me whatever you will in My kingdom and in My infinite treasury. If it is for your benefit, you shall have it." Ask for whatever you need. Ask for temporal things, and they will be yours, if they are for your good. But ask earnestly for the Spirit, and spiritual things, and there is no danger of offending Him. You shall have. He will give you eternal life according to His promise. And you must have the Spirit before you can enter life or be fitted for it.

If natural fathers are good to their children, God is a better Father. He can give better gifts. This Father is the author of every kind and gentle affection in all other fathers. This Father is better than all, more tender in heart, more ready to hear, more able to give, infinitely greater in His person and in His gifts. We have, therefore, every encouragement to be fervent and persistent in prayer. Let us pray earnestly for the Spirit.

III. Some general exhortations to pray for the Spirit

First, since the Father has given the Son, why should He not also give the Spirit? This is a powerful argument and a firm basis for believing that He will do so. "He that spared not his own Son, but delivered him up for us all, how shall he not with him freely give us all things?" (Rom. 8:32). The first gift has opened the way for the second. The Father gave the Son, and that is ground for expecting Him to fulfill His promise regarding the Spirit. The love of the Father was so great that He gave His Son, and He gave the Son to open the way for the Spirit, that sinners might come freely by faith in His blood to the Father's throne.

Second, the Son has the Spirit to give Him, and now He does give Him. He is called the Spirit of Christ, and all authority is in the hand of Christ. Jesus now has immense power at the right hand of the Father, and He is able to give the Spirit. Ask for Him, and ask earnestly. I am afraid of teaching you to presume, and causing graceless men to act as spiritual, but if you are not a hypocrite, and find yourself in a fitting state, say these words, "O God, give me Thy Spirit, and do not refuse me. Unless Thou givest me Thy Spirit

Thou wilt not fulfill Thy purpose, Thou wilt not be true to Thy promises, and the everlasting covenant will have been in vain. Thou wilt lose not only Thy children, but Thy glory as well. The eternal plan will collapse in confusion. Blessed Jesus, Thy purpose when thou wast nailed to the cross and died at Calvary was too high to be allowed to be in vain. Why didst Thou come to the world and die, give the gospel to be proclaimed, raise preachers, provide the means of grace, and prescribe the ordinances if Thou didst not intend to send the Spirit to give them effect? I beseech Thee, give Thy Spirit. Thy death will have no purpose without the Spirit, and Thy blood, however much merit there is in it, will have been shed in vain unless He applies it. Unless He is given, Thy coming to the world will have been to no avail. Apart from this, the whole church is expecting Him, and we have every encouragement to believe He is to be had. Thy servants can do no good, nor can Thy people fulfill any duty without Him."

And so, let zealous, persistent prayer find its way from this church to heaven, and let our petitions in the name of the Righteous ascend like incense for the Spirit. If He does not come, the work of salvation will never be fulfilled. But we do not have to be satisfied without Him. He is needed and He is to be had. He has been promised to convince the world of sin, and to take of the things of Christ to show to sinners. He has been promised to remove the veil, and to teach the unlearned and to make the foolish wise unto salvation. It will be to the glory of God to send the Spirit, and it will be a foretaste of heaven to the saints on earth. God promises His Spirit, and sometimes gives Him to those who do not seek Him. How much more will He give the Spirit to them who do seek Him? Whatever your need, ask for the Holy Spirit, because this includes everything. Whatever the poor and weak want to do for God, He will be given the means to do it by the Spirit. He will have strength from Him if he is weak. He will have strength to believe, strength to love Him, strength to obey. Here he will have the means to walk in all God's commandments. Through the Spirit he will be enabled to overcome enemies, and to resist the temptations that ensnared him. He will do all these things. There is nothing lacking that He cannot supply, nothing difficult for which He cannot give strength, no danger from which He cannot deliver, no comfort that He cannot give. He will be your helper and comforter. He will be your guide unto death, and with you in death, when all others have forsaken you; He will seal you until the day of redemption.

And now I close by exhorting you to seek Him. Ask for Him. Ask at all times. Ask earnestly. Ask without fainting. Ask for your own good and everyone else's, and for the benefit of the entire world. Ask for the Spirit for yourself and for your neighbors and for the whole world, for their good and for their salvation.

In every distress, affliction, agony and darkness, in every circumstance of adversity, confusion, and depression that meets you, call on, and ask for the Holy Spirit. Yes, and on your deathbed ask for Him for yourself and for the whole earth. You need not fear that He will be offended, and there is no danger of asking too much or too often. Ask as much as you like, and however often you ask, your Father will not be offended, and He will never tire of listening.

After you have asked for Him, expect Him. Do not let your weakness be a hindrance. Go to Him in your poverty to lead you from your poverty, and to heaven itself.

O infinite God, pour out a spirit of prayer on the people until we have an outpouring of Thy Spirit among them. Show the people their wicked condition, show them Thy salvation, and incline thousands to embrace Thee and Thy Spirit, for Christ's sake. Amen.

The Greatness of the Peace of God, which is Above Understanding

"And the peace of God, which passes all understanding, shall keep your hearts and minds through Christ Jesus."
—Philippians 4:7

True ministers of the gospel in every age, being sent by God, love their hearers deeply. They excel all others in the love they have for the souls of their hearers. It may be that ministers who are not sent by God may be better scholars than those who are sent—perhaps they are more amusing, more eloquent speakers, more fluent orators, more able in the way they handle a subject. But here lies the excellence of true ministers: they love the glory of God and the good of their people more than their own honor and ease and reputation. If a minister of the gospel loves something in himself, or seeks his own ends rather than the glory of God, that man is not of God. Paul loved his hearers greatly and was ready to spend and to be spent for their souls, although they loved him the less, as he declares to the Corinthians (2 Cor. 12:15). He had a particular love for some more than others, those among whom he had enjoyed the most fellowship with God. There was more of a closeness between him and those among whom he found more of God. So it was with these Philippians. He was exceptionally near to them from the day he first had fellowship with them until the day he wrote this letter. He is hopeful that the good work begun in them will be continued until the day of Christ.

In the third chapter of this letter the apostle relates his experience, like a preacher to his listeners. "What things were gain to me, those I counted loss for Christ" (Phil. 3:7). Thus he continued to regard them without any regret. "Yea doubtless, and I count all things but loss for the excellency of the knowledge of Christ Jesus my

Lord: for whom I have suffered the loss of all things, and do count them but dung, that I may win Christ" (v. 8). He was also thirsting for perfection, while recognizing that he had not reached perfection, but was aiming for it, forgetting the things that were behind him and pressing forward for what lay ahead. Then he expresses his concern because of the way some religious people were conducting themselves. So overcome was he by this that he wept as he wrote and called them the enemies of the cross of Christ.

And these were religious people! The immoral lives of the pagans and Mohammedans are not nearly as bad as the ungodliness of professing Christians. No one's ungodly life strikes so directly at the cross of Christ as does the ungodly life of someone who professes to be His follower. "Whose end is destruction"—although they have a profession—"whose God is their belly, and whose glory is in their shame" (Phil. 3:19). Their concern is with the things of earth. In contrast, he shows what kind of life the Christian lives. "Our conversation is in heaven"—it is that country's language that we speak, it is to that country that we are traveling, we have the stamp of that country upon us, it is for that country that we thirst, and from there we expect the Savior, the Lord Jesus Christ. Then He will raise us from the grave in His image. "Therefore, stand fast in the Lord"—to await the morning. Stand without bringing shame on religion, stand without being discouraged in the face of persecutions, stand without falling before false professors, stand fast in the Lord. "I beseech Euodias, and beseech Syntyche, that they be of the same mind in the Lord. And I intreat thee also, true yokefellow, help those women" (Phil. 4:2). Help them to be reconciled to each other. They are weaker vessels, and are worth caring for because "they labored with me." "Rejoice in the Lord alway: and again I say, Rejoice. Let your moderation be known unto all men" (Phil. 4:4-5). By moderation, he means them to be sensible, temperate, gentle, and not to be angry. And in order to provoke them to this he says, "The Lord is at hand."

Two ways we can understand this text are as follows: the Lord is at hand watching you, and the time is at hand when He will come to judge the world. Therefore, do not seek vengeance, but leave all avenging to Him. "Be careful for nothing; but in everything by prayer and supplication with thanksgiving let your requests be made known unto God" (v. 6).

So we come to the text, "And the peace of God, which passes all understanding, shall keep your hearts and minds through Christ Jesus" (v. 7). As you walk this way and observe my advice, you will experience peace with God. This peace will keep you in tribulation and in ease, in temptations and perils, through Christ Jesus. Then he gives them extremely comprehensive counsel. "Finally, brethren, whatsoever things are true, whatsoever things are honest, whatsoever things are just, whatsoever things are pure, whatsoever things are lovely, whatsoever things are of good report; if there be any virtue, and if there be any praise, think on these things" (v. 8). Strive after the best things to be had on earth—the best in doctrine, the best in experience, the best in your manner of life, the best in your families, the best in your neighborhoods, and the best in the church. Seek the best in every respect. Do not be content with the knowledge that there is one virtue in the human condition, nor one feature worthy of praise on the face of the earth, that is not in your possession. If you know of any virtue in temperament, in speech, in life, in family, in the neighborhood, in business, or in employment belonging to any man on earth, do not rest until you make it yours. "Those things, which you have both learned, and received, and heard, and seen in me, do" (v. 9). If you see any merit or virtue in anyone, learn from him. Even if the man is the most ungodly in other respects, if there is any worthy feature in him, be instructed by him. Learn virtue even from evil, by doing the opposite. Let there be no Christian lacking one virtue. "And the God of peace shall be with you" (v. 9). In this way not only will the peace of God be with you, but the very God of that peace. I draw your attention to three matters in the text.

I. What the apostle was speaking about: the peace of God
II. The greatness of the peace of God: which passeth all understanding

III. The merit and effects of this peace: shall keep your
      hearts and minds through Christ Jesus

I. The peace of God

All peace is good except peace with Satan. I do not know of
any bad peace apart from this. The Bible speaks in one place of the
strong man armed who keeps his goods in peace. That is bad peace.
Every other form of peace is good. There is peace between countries, peace within kingdoms between ruler and citizens, peace
between neighbors, peace within a household, peace between
brothers, and personal peace in the heart, and all of them are
extremely valuable. There is nothing more profitable, precious, and
delightful than these kinds of peace. How terrible is the slaughter
on the field of battle when peace is forfeited between two countries!
How wretched is the hell that is let loose in the homes where peace
is lacking. Many do not have this peace, and their hearts are filled
with fear. This is a peace of such value that it is beyond my power
to describe; it is beyond all understanding. But it is a peace greater
than all—"The peace of God." If the peace of men is so precious,
how much more precious is the peace of God! I shall consider this
peace in two ways: what peace with God means, and the peace that
God made.

First, peace with God is the root and foundation of all other
peace. There is no continuing peace between anyone unless it
springs from the peace of God.

1. Men by nature do not have this peace. They are enemies of God;
God is angry with them, and whets His sword against them. It is
while we were enemies that Christ died for us, enemies in thought
and deed. Anger, malice, poison, and implacable, destructive bitterness, all directed against God, are found in the sinner's heart, and
the wrath of God is kindled against the ungodly. His arrows are set
to the bow, and they are aimed at the ungodly. "There is no peace,
saith my God, to the wicked" (Isa. 57:21). There is contention
between sinners and God, and that enmity breaks out in hatred
against the gospel of God, the cause of God, the people of God,

and the Christ of God. God's enmity is directed against them, not as His creatures, but as those who have broken His law, and have opposed His government and nature. They are rebels. Unless we see how dreadful this hostility against God is, we shall not see the value of His mercy. We in this country who have been brought up in peace do not know the worth of peace. On the other hand, the Spanish know a great deal of its value in these days, since they are forced to leave their homes, escape from their country out of fear of their enemies, and are in danger every day because of the oppression of the Corsican Bonaparte.

2. In spite of this, God is the God of peace, although He is the enemy of the ungodly. It was not God who began the quarrel. God does not change and He cannot be turned. It is man who transgressed, who rebelled, and who became an enemy. The continuance of the enmity is from man's side. But God had thoughts of peace toward man from the beginning of the world. For this reason there was a covenant of peace and a council of peace between the Father and the Son, even before the conflict.

3. God sent His Son into the world to effect reconciliation between the two parties, to suffer the just punishment instead of the wrongdoer, and to secure for men peace with God.

4. God sends His Spirit to convict, to humble and to bend sinners, to prepare them for the peace of God, and to make them ready to receive reconciliation. He reveals His Son to them, and the peace that He won; He draws men to the Son that they may receive Him, and so receive reconciliation. By receiving Christ they can say, "We have peace with God." Second, peace is the work of God. Notice three things here: peace in the conscience, peace with men, and peace in respect of providence, that is, a calmness of soul in the face of the providences of God.

Peace of conscience springs from the awareness of peace with God. This is not the unfeeling drowsiness that is careless and unconcerned and knows nothing of fear because of ignorance of the situation between man and God. That is nothing other than sheer atheism. The peace of which we speak is the result of knowing peace with God. The conscience will never be at peace apart from reconciliation with God. You can lull the conscience and sear the conscience, but you cannot still it without peace with God. God is content with the atonement, in the sacrifice of His Son. Our sins were laid to His account.

Righteousness and the law are at peace with the sinner in the sacrifice at Calvary. And I, too, am satisfied, says the conscience. The conscience can be sleepy, undisturbed, indifferent, and seared, but there is no such thing as peace of conscience apart from peace with God.

Those who have peace with God have an appetite for peace in every place, especially with other men. If anybody strikes one of these on his cheek, he will turn the other to him. And if anyone takes his coat, he will give him his cloak also for the sake of peace. They are called the sons of peace. They take pleasure in peace; it is their natural element. They want to live at peace not only with the saints, but with all men, godly and ungodly alike—not indeed with their ungodliness and their sins but with their persons. Sons of peace are peacemakers, gentle, meek, and modest.

They also have peace in respect of providence. This means to be quiet under the providences of God, to murmur their complaint to Him in prayer. Are they therefore heedless of their condition? Certainly not, but they are aware of their weakness. Your unreasonable anxieties cannot add one cubit to your stature; and for all your worrying, you cannot make one hair black or white. These believe this truth; they see their feebleness and their defects, and they say, "Let us go like children to our Father, and make our situation known to Him." They pour out their hearts before Him, and then are able to be at peace. They call on the Lord, they wait on the Lord, and trust Him in every circumstance; yes, they trust Him even if there is no sheep in the fold, nor oxen in the stable. By pouring their hearts out before God in their distress, they have victory in their affliction, and a way to be quiet in the fiercest storm. Instead of complaining in their trouble, they wait on the Lord, and trust in God, who rules in everything. The Christian says, "If the providence of God was so oppressive that there were no sheep in the fold or cattle in the stable, or if the hills were removed and the mountains carried into the midst of the sea, I will be glad in the Lord, and rejoice in the God of my salvation." The people who have peace with God are at peace with His providence. They will not be afraid in the face of all the changes of nature, because their hope is securely founded. The peace of God in the soul creates such a peace among all the providences of God that it can face even the king of terrors and say with David, "Though I walk through the valley of the shadow of death, I will fear no evil." Those in possession of this peace can be subdued like Aaron, and bow meekly like Eli, even if God should kill their children. They are able to say with Job, "Blessed be the name of the Lord," though He should take from them all their wealth (Job 1:21). They are silent and compliant, no matter what they receive at the hand of their God and Father.

The experience of the peace of God enables a man to submit to all the ways in which God deals with him, and the manner in which He rules the world. He is meek and without any resentment, however bitter the affliction with which God visits him. The sight of God at peace with them turns the most severe providence into a feast. When Christians are tried and tested by the world to the limit of their endurance they remember that Jesus their husband has overcome the world, and they cry in triumph, "In all these things we are more than conquerors through him that loved us" (Rom. 8:37). God keeps in perfect peace the minds of all who trust in Him. In the peace of God we have peace even with the animals, peace with every creature except the devils, all through the sovereignty of our Father and God.

II. The greatness of the peace
     "The peace of God, which passes all understanding." This peace is beyond the grasp of created beings. The people who do not have this peace with God are to be pitied more than anyone. Men and women who are yet without the peace of God, and who are not

accepted in the Beloved, you cannot begin to understand your miserable condition. There is nothing worse in the world than to be destitute of the peace of God. Whatever is your standing in the world, if you were to inherit all the kingdoms of the earth, and were to be without this, you would be the poorest of men, and the most pitiable person on earth. No poverty or illness imaginable can be compared with this wretchedness. No want of bread, no sickness, no humiliation, no poverty, or any temporal distress is for a moment to be compared with this. It is better not to have any of God's mercies than not to have His peace. To have it is an indescribable privilege. It is beyond understanding because it is perfect, and our small minds cannot embrace perfection.

This peace is beyond finite understanding. It surpasses understanding in its nature, in its ordering and arrangement, and in its fitness and design. The peace of God is above all understanding. It goes beyond the understanding of every kind of man, and every kind of knowledge.

Furthermore, it is especially beyond the understanding of those who have not experienced it. This person knows nothing about it. No one who does not have the peace and who has not experienced it has the slightest idea of what it is, and does not believe that such a thing exists. Because he does not know about it, he does not believe that anyone knows about it. He thinks those who claim it are fanatics or enthusiasts. He thinks the man who knows something about it from experience, and who rejoices in its possession is a fool. There is no point in speaking to him about such a thing because he does not believe that there is such a thing. However, whether men understand or not, it does exist, and it is to be had today by all who seek it. All men are either at peace with God or at enmity: they know His smile or His frown.

There are two kinds of people in the world. There is scarcely any gathering of people that does not contain those at peace with God and those at enmity with Him mingled together. No doubt it is like that in this delightful congregation. Some of this company are now under the wrath of God, and some are in His favor. Those who know His favor need not be afraid if the judgment were to come tomorrow, but it is different with those who do not know anything about the peace of God and are not aware of their need. Often our telling them of a way of peace with God is nothing but foolishness to them. To them, ministers and missionaries are merely mocking and joking. When we call upon them to be reconciled and warn them to escape from their danger, they think we are either amusing or fanatical.

This peace is past the understanding of all men. No kind of knowledge of art or science will enable a man to come to terms with the meaning of the peace of God. Many skilled and learned astronomers can tell you how far away the sun is and how large it is, and can give you a detailed description of all the planets. They can tell you the number of miles there are from here to Venus, Saturn, and Mars, and how each revolves on its axis, the rate at which they travel and the vast distances they cover. But if these men, with all their wisdom, are not reconciled to God, then the poor, uneducated godly man knows more about the peace of God than the scholar, since it is beyond the knowledge of all who have not experienced it.

The man who does not have the peace of God does not want the peace of God because he does not know its worth. It is of no account to him, and he has no appetite or taste for it. His mind is entirely on the things of earth. He prefers to talk about anything rather than the peace of God. All kinds of knowledge and gifts are more important to him than this. It is almost impossible to get him to consider the vital question: does he have peace with God?

The man who has no experience of the peace of God knows no more about it than the animals. Those who live only for the flesh know no more about spiritual things than does an animal about natural things. It is just as well to ask a donkey to describe the sun as to ask you to describe the peace of God. Only those who are of God can discern the things that are of the Spirit of God because "they are spiritually discerned." Indeed, I find myself being driven to pray for them and to cry, "O God, have mercy on this people, and whatever Thou doest to them, bring them to that state where they know Thy peace."

Third, the peace of God passes the knowledge even of those who have experienced it. These know something about it, but not all. They know in part, but as yet, not perfectly. The peace of God, like the love of God, is unsearchable. No one knows it to perfection. No one perfectly knows its length, breadth, height, or depth. What was said about another matter can with equal propriety be said about this: "Eye hath not seen, nor ear heard, neither have entered into the heart of man" (1 Cor. 2:9), even the thousandth part of the completeness of the peace of God. Those who know most know little; and those who see most clearly, see little of the wonder of the peace of God. When those with the most acute faculties and the greatest achievements see most clearly, and are given most light and the greatest revelations, when they are given the most powerful telescopes to gaze through the darkness at this indescribable wonder, they must at the end confess that it surpasses their understanding. At last they can do nothing but stand before it and say, "Amazing!" It is a wonder and an astonishment to us. It is too high. Who can understand it, discern it, or relate it?

The peace of God passes all understanding in three respects:

1. In terms of its root cause
2. In terms of its order and beginning
3. In terms of its application to the need of the soul

1. It exceeds all ability to understand it when we think of what occasioned it. Nothing other than the free, unconstrained, eternal love with which God loved sinners! Why, asks the inquisitive soul, did the great God think about such a weak, poor, and wicked creature such as I am? Why did His free grace run past more deserving creatures in pursuit of such a miserable object? Why did He not leave me, like the fallen angels, bound in chains of darkness until the great day of judgment? Why did He not abandon me to what I deserved, to be left without mercy in my misery, and to be punished without sparing for all eternity for my sin? It is impossible to say

why. All we can say is that it is a wonder to men and angels, a wonder beyond understanding!

2. It passes understanding in respect of its ordering. Who can understand the depth of the love and grace that sent the Son into the world to take our nature, and to humble Himself, placing Himself under our sins, to suffer and die in our place? It is an inexhaustible source of wonder that the Son should be sent and humbled, and in this way, open a way for sin to be punished and sinners to be saved. The sacrifice is slain that the guilty may be spared. The surety is stricken that there may be a way for the wrongdoer to go free. "The chastisement of our peace was upon him; and with his stripes we are healed" (Isa. 53:5). He submitted to being killed that we might live. He took the punishment for our peace that the peace might be ours. Through His bruises and His death, peace and life come to all those who believe in Him. In the face of this, men and angels are drowned in amazement to see the Prince of peace stooping so low and taking human nature, subjecting himself to sinners' weakness and shame, and for their sakes enduring intense agony and death. What righteousness and everlasting release He won for them on the ground of His atonement! The preciousness of His blood and the merit of His sacrifice are an ocean of wonders that cannot be contained or grasped, and a depth that no creature can measure or plumb. Its beginning is outside our ability to comprehend. When was the peace made? How did it originate? "All I know," says someone, "is that once I was wild, but I was caught in the gospel net." Another says, "It was in such and such a meeting that I was brought to my senses by some power unseen by me. This conviction was so painful that I thought at first that God wanted to damn me. Now I see that His intention was to bring me to His peace. When I thought that He was destroying me and taking my life, I was being given medicine to reveal to me the author of peace." Peace has been made; but its ordering is a source of infinite astonishment to us.

3. The peace of God is wonderful in its nature, its application to the

need of the soul, and the experience of it in the soul. In its essence, it is a sweet sense of the calm of God in the soul, an appreciation of His love and grace, full contentment with the ordering and the means of reconciliation. It is the soul resting on the sacrifice of Christ and finding its repose in the offering, the blood, and the sinless sacrifice that was made on the cross, and the salvation that was completed there.

What is the peace of God? It is to look on God as your dear Father, and on Jesus as your loving and cherished brother, and on the Holy Spirit as your guide and supreme comforter. It is to look on His peace as your heaven forever. Your perfect peace is to see God as your faithful Creator, and Jesus Christ as your all-sufficient Savior.

The peace of God will keep you under the fiery thunders of Sinai, and in all the afflictions and distresses of the wilderness. It will lift up your head in death, sustain you in the judgment, and will accompany you to the other side. It will remain in the soul when the tabernacle is destroyed. When the pillars of the soul are removed, the beauty will be preserved. When the soul flies to glory, God's peace will be undisturbed. It produces a sweetness you cannot describe. It is beyond understanding in the experience of the soul.

I cannot leave this subject without speaking clearly and calling urgently to those whose delight is in the pleasures of the flesh. Oh, children of the flesh! Where are you with your husks? You have no idea what enjoyment is. A mere drop of the peace of God is worth more than a sea of your pleasures, and a mountain of the experience of the peace of God than all the delights the universe has to offer. One Christian has more delight in one minute from the experience of the peace of God than ten thousand of you have in ages of worldly pleasures. Again, the peace of God is past man's understanding in its value. Who can count the thousandth part of its worth? Who shall I ask? Not the atheist. Poor man, he does not know that such a thing exists. He is like the man blind from birth, who, because he has never seen the light denies that there is such a thing. It is no good to ask the skeptic or the doubter. He does not believe that God is to be trusted. Nor is there any purpose served by asking the formal professor or hypocrite. It is no worse to ask a donkey for a description of this peace than to ask this man. He knows nothing about it. But here is a man who has been under the shadow of Sinai, who has been convicted of his lost condition, and realizes that God is angry with the ungodly. He is aware of his grim danger and dreadful condition if he remains within the reach of the sword of God. So deeply has he felt his distress that he has almost been driven mad, and has tried his utmost to save himself, but failed. He has tried to pay his debt, and to make himself clean, and to make himself better. Indeed he has tried to raise himself from the dead, gain the peace of God, and earn his salvation. But he has completely failed, and instead of improving, he has become much, much worse. This is the man whose refuge was sunk beneath the waters, and whose frail shelter was swept away by the flood of divine conviction. As far as he is concerned, his end has come. His heart has been pricked; his legal hopes have been struck a mortal blow. The sword of the Spirit of God has come, sharper than any two-edged sword, and divided his soul and his spirit. This is the man to ask what is the value of the peace of God. But although he knows so much, he himself confesses that he cannot tell you. He cannot speak of what he has experienced and felt of its worth, not even a fraction. It is indescribable and incomprehensible, like its author. It truly passes all understanding, and goes beyond the ability of any creature to grasp. There is nothing visible or invisible to be compared with it.

Well, then, is there no way in which we can have it? Yes, blessed be God. It is to be had, and is within the reach of poor men and women like those who are here today. It is within reach—the God of peace gives it, He who rules over everything. And when His peace is experienced, the wildest storm in the most troubled soul is stilled. I have been in distress, says the convicted soul, until my legal hope was dead, and I myself was finished. But the God of peace gave me peace. Therefore, to Him I will turn in every extremity. His peace alone can silence the troubled soul, and will minister comfort

in the valley of the shadow of death. Its worth transcends understanding, and cannot be imagined, grasped, or conceived. For this
reason, to seek to describe it would be to darken counsel. This is
"the peace of God, which passes all understanding."

III. The virtues and effects of this peace

"Shall keep your hearts and minds through Christ Jesus." Oh, what
rich grace! It keeps the heart in Christ. I shall not look in detail at
the meaning of what it is to keep the heart, but only in general. I
take the word "heart" to mean all the faculties of the soul. The
Greek for "keep" here means to "garrison" or "guard." However
you read the words, they are full of comfort: the peace of God will
keep guard over your hearts; or the peace of God will be guard in
your hearts and souls; or the peace of God will keep your hearts in
Christ Jesus as in a castle or fort. To be kept in this peace has
immense value. The peace of God will keep your hearts from sinning; it will keep you from being discouraged, from falling or
turning back, from changing or falling from the grace of God. In
this you have been made to hope. Do not rely on anything to keep
the soul but what God has ordered, nor on anything to comfort it
but the precious peace of God. By the heart is meant the whole
man, and to keep the heart is to keep the whole man. If it is well
with your heart, it will be well with all the members of your body.
If your soul is with God, all your members will promote the glory
of God. The eyes, the ears, the hands and the feet will all be united
to this end. "The peace of God...shall keep your hearts and minds"
in the following ways:

1. It will keep them from sinning. But will not the fear of hell do
this? No! Unless you have the peace of God, you would sin, even
in the flames. The fear of hell, and even the fierce wrath of God,
however dreadful, will not stop anyone from sinning against Him,
because men still sin against Him in hell. If there was a way for the
fiery waves of hell to wash over the earth and carry some back from
Gehenna to have a second opportunity, without the grace of God
they would sin even then. The fear of hell and the wrath of God do

not change the sinner in the least, nor convert his soul. All they do is restrain him for a little while out of fear of being punished. After that, he breaks out into sin as violently as before. As long as man does not have a new nature, sin reigns in him, and therefore his inclination is toward sin. The peace of God alone is sufficient to restrain sin. The peace of God reconciles the man who possesses it to the law of God, by showing him a way to come up to its demands, and to answer to its curses, through Him who made an end of it in his place. The convicted soul now feels such a celestial peace that he comes to keep the law instead of breaking it. The peace of God is the best antidote to sin. To be reconciled to God will reconcile us to His law. A sight of Him as the God of peace, and an experience of His peace will do more than anything to mortify sin. The gift and the grace overcome sin. What is the lesson we learn from this? Shall we sin that grace may abound? God forbid!

2. The peace of God is the best protection against discouragement and fainting, from falling in our thoughts and letting go of the religion of the Son of God. If we have to meet with storms and tempests, care and weariness, and fiery temptations, in those bitter circumstances it is the peace of God that is best fitted to preserve our minds, keep us from falling, fainting, and relaxing our hold. It will save us from being disheartened and giving up, and will strengthen us in our resolve to persevere through fire and water, determined never to turn back. This peace is a great encouragement to go on. In the strength of this, we can go on through everything quietly, uncomplainingly, willingly, full of a godly jealousy, intent on gaining life, and refusing to turn back.

Let me speak, finally, to three kinds of people. First, to those who do not as yet have the peace of God. There is not one kind of ministry that has any effect on you. It is better to pray for you than to speak to you. I might as well address the woods or the wall as address you. Dear unhappy and pitiful people, you are in such a wretched state! You are without peace with God, and yet you feel no urgency to seek that peace. Perhaps you never saw it worth falling on your knees to seek, nor to ask God for. You are able to go to bed and to get up, to lie down and sleep quietly and heedlessly, with the sword of God hanging over your head, and the wrath of the Infinite One against you like a whirlwind, approaching nearer and nearer. If it reaches you, woe, woe, woe to you forever! If you are given a little longer on earth, use it with all your might to seek peace with God, and do not go to your deathbed for anything without it. Beware of trusting in a sigh or a prayer a few minutes before you die. Do not trust in anything as unsure as a deathbed religion or last-minute prayer. Even if you could be certain of them, they are the most unfavorable occasions of all. Perhaps by then your senses will be utterly confused, and if not, there will be enough confusion of other sorts—the intense pains of death, the awakened conscience, the accusations of Satan, the heavens darkening and raging dreadfully above your head, and you without any escape. For your soul's sake, hasten, come to the Savior, while you are well, and in the day of grace. Come to God to seek His peace in the face of Jesus Christ, that it may be well with you in death. Then, and only then, will you see the value of the peace of God that passes understanding.

On the other hand, no one can tell how sad it will be to see you in the valley, outside of the peace of God. The thought of your pains, your sighing, your hopeless screams, pierces my soul like arrows, and your shouting and lamenting, "Why did I not learn, and listen to the voice of my teachers, and know the things that belonged to my peace? Now they are hidden from me! For me the preaching of the gospel has finished. I will never again hear the sound of the ministry of reconciliation. The door of mercy has been shut against me forever, and I am without the peace of God and without any hope at all!"

Oh dear people, I pray that none in this lovely gathering will be found at last in those sad circumstances. However, I am delighted to tell you all today, that it is not yet so. I have a message from God to deliver to you on His behalf. "Be ye reconciled to God" (2 Cor. 5:20). You, blackest sinners, rebels, enemies, the most arrogant and stubborn, the hardest and worst on the face of the earth, come to Christ as you are, to be transformed and cleansed. You may have perfect reconciliation. The day of grace is not ended.

Second, let me speak to those religious people who do not know whether they have peace with God or not. It is a very dangerous thing to go into the other world with a religion without knowing if it is of the right kind. Will it endure in the day of judgment? How will it appear in the scales of justice on the last day? What is the good of being an aged follower of religion, if it is nothing but a dry and rotten trunk? Sinner on your way to judgment and to a long eternity, not knowing whether your religion will be in vain at last, insist on knowing, and although you cannot reach that knowledge on your own, go to God to experience it. Call on Him, saying, "Search me, O God, and know my heart: try me, and know my thoughts: and see if there be any wicked way in me, and lead me in the way everlasting" (Ps. 139:23-25).

Lastly, you who have experienced this peace, magnify the God of the peace. Thank Him for His goodness and bless Him for His unspeakable gift. Pray that you may be kept in the way and enjoy His peace. Amen.

Funeral Sermon of King George III

The following essay contains the substance of what I preached on the occasion of the death of our gracious king, George III. It is not because I thought that there was any particular virtue in it that I agreed to its appearance in print, but because I thought it necessary that people should be shown the relationship that exists between subjects and their king, and the duty of subjects to respect, submit to, and obey him in everything conformable to the Word of God. I also saw that the people of Britain were under a great obligation to honor the memory of His Majesty George III, and that the people of Wales were as much indebted to him as any others in the nation. It is for this reason that I acceded to the request of certain of my friends to publish the substance of what I preached on that occasion. I have added some facts and features that I gleaned from the most accurate accounts available to me, chiefly in regard to morality, virtue, and religion, leaving to one side political issues, it being outside the scope of my responsibility to deal with them. If this meager tribute to the memory of His Majesty is received by my countrymen, I will consider that as a mark of their esteem for his memory more than of the insignificant author of this essay—and that is my purpose.

John Elias
Llanfechell
April 15, 1820

"And he died, and was buried in one of the sepulchers of his fathers. And all Judah and Jerusalem mourned for Josiah. And Jeremiah lamented for Josiah: and all the singing men and the singing women spoke of Josiah in their lamentations to this day."
—2 Chronicles 35:24, 25

Men of a broad and unambitious spirit take the cause of others to their hearts. They rejoice in the success of their neighbors and their nation, and they mourn in their distress and tribulation. Selfish men care only for their own personal affairs. The Christian is a man who is for his nation. He thinks of his nation as his family and himself as one of the family, as a body and himself as a member of the body. Any injury, wound, or pain in any part of the body, especially the head, affects him. The death of those who are useful and famous in the country is a source of grief and anxiety to everyone. The Christian is affected in this way and feels the loss deeply. Isaiah complained that "the righteous perishes, and no man lays it to heart: and merciful men are taken away, none considering that the righteous is taken away from the evil to come" (Isa. 57:1). The death of a good, gentle, godly king is a cause of great sadness to the nation in general and to the godly in particular. Thus was the death of Josiah to all Judah, and especially to Jeremiah.

Solomon said that it was an evil under the sun that the same thing happens to all men. The great and the good, the righteous and the honorable die just like the weak, the foolish and the wicked. Death is the way of all the earth and the grave "the house appointed for all living" (Job 30:23). So Josiah, though famous and godly, died. Although he was wounded on the battlefield, he went to the grave in peace according to the word of Huldah the prophetess, "Thou shalt be gathered to thy grave in peace" (2 Chron. 34:28). He went to the grave at peace with God, at peace with his conscience, and at peace with his subjects. He was buried "in one of the sepulchers of his fathers," an honor not given to every king. It is said of King Jehoram, "He departed without being desired" (2 Chron. 21:20). "His people made no burning for him, like the burning of his fathers" (2 Chron. 21:19). About Jehoiakim the son of Josiah we read, "They shall not lament for him...he shall be buried with the burial of an ass" (Jer. 22:18). The king of Babylon was warned that he would not lie in the same grave as the kings of the nations. They would lie in glory, each one in his own house, that is, the grave, but he would be like a trampled corpse. Similarly, Richard III in England, who seized the crown by killing his two nephews—within two years and two months, was himself killed, and his corpse was carried naked on a horse, like a butcher taking an animal to market. His body was left lying exposed for two days in Leicester without being buried. But Josiah was buried.

When we consider the account of Josiah, it is not surprising that he was given such an honorable burial and that he was so deeply mourned. Let us remember these features. He was mentioned by name in prophecy many years before he was born. During Jeroboam's days the work he would do was described in detail, "O, altar, altar, thus says the Lord; behold, a child shall be born unto the house of David, Josiah by name; and upon thee shall he offer the priests of the high places that burn incense upon thee, and men's bones shall be burnt upon thee" (1 Kings 13:2). He began to reign when he was eight years old, and he did what was right in the eyes of the Lord—he did not incline to the right or to the left. When he was sixteen years old he was given a supernatural experience of God so that he began to seek the God of David his father more publicly. When he was twenty he began to purge Jerusalem of the high places, the groves, and the idols. So fierce was his zeal against idolatry that he burnt the bones of the idolatrous priests on their altars. This he did not only in Judah, but also throughout Israel. It seems that the king of Babylon allowed him to do this. He had extended his borders far beyond his fathers, and in his entire kingdom he sought to destroy idolatry and promote the worship of the true God. He pulled down the altar in Bethel that Jeroboam had erected, thus fulfilling the prophecy. Probably his desire to destroy that one was greater, since it was the fountain of all the idol-worship in Israel, one of the two which Jeroboam had built to seduce the people away from the true God. He was also consumed with a passion to tear down completely the high places of Solomon and the altars of Manasseh, indeed all the remains of the corruption of the kings who had been before him.

In the eighteenth year of his reign he began to repair the temple of the Lord. At that time the high priest discovered the book of the law of the Lord, and Shaphan the scribe read it before the king, who tore his clothes on hearing it, and his heart was softened. He sent for Huldah the prophetess in his distress because he saw the curses contained in the book, and the wrath of God on the land. The prophetess said that he should go to the grave in peace because his heart was softened.

Josiah was remarkable for reforming the land from its immorality. He threw down the houses of the sodomites, took away the detestable idols from the territory, renewed the covenant between the people and God, and walked in the way of the Lord. He observed the Passover, the like of which had never been seen before. We have a perfect description of Josiah in 2 Kings 23:25, "And like unto him was there no king before him, that turned to the Lord with all his heart, and with all his soul, and with all his might, according to all the law of Moses; neither after him arose there any like him." He began to follow the Lord while he was young, and he increased in zeal and faithfulness as he increased in age. His heart was tender and his hatred of sin immense.

After reigning prosperously and successfully for thirty-one years, Josiah was killed in the valley of Megiddo fighting against Necho, the king of Egypt. Josiah may have been too impulsive in going to this battle; he should have been more cautious and consulted with God more. What a pity that there is a blemish on the name of Josiah, who had led such a good and blameless life in the cause of God! No doubt we should be wary of finding greater fault with him than the Bible does. It is probable that Josiah was bound to go to war because of a treaty made with the king of Babylon, who had been kind to him in allowing him to rule over Israel. Megiddo was in the land of Israel, and Necho was trying to go through that land against the king of Babylon, so Josiah felt obliged to oppose him. He received a fatal wound in the battle, and by that deadly arrow, Judah was bereft of its outstanding godly king. "And he died"—and no wonder that there was such mourning for him, mourning without its like, "the mourning of Hadadrimmon in the valley of Megiddon" (Zech. 12:11).

Great men had been mourned before. They mourned for Jacob the father of the Israelite nation for seventy days; for Moses the leader and deliverer of Israel thirty days; for Aaron the priest of the nation thirty days; for Samuel their judge, all of Israel mourned. David mourned grievously after Saul and Jonathan; all Israel mourned for Abiah because there was found some good in him toward the Lord God of Israel. But the mourning for Josiah was greatest.

I. All Israel mourned, all the inhabitants of the country, near and far. The effects of his good rule reached all levels of society throughout the land. He was like a tender and caring father to all the family of Judah, and they were like orphans mourning for him.

II. All Jerusalem mourned for him. His virtues were evident in the city, and his praise was no less near his palace. The priests in the temple and the princes in the courts knew Josiah's worth, and they mourned for him.

III. Jeremiah, the great prophet of God, who flattered no man, mourned for Josiah. A virtuous king is a great encouragement to godly prophets to stand against the corruption of the age and for the service and glory of God. So did Jeremiah account of Josiah, and realized the consequences of losing him. With a heavy heart and a distressed soul he mourned because of the consequences.

IV. The men and women singers in their laments constantly remembered him. Perhaps as they sang of the merits of someone else, they would remember the merits of Josiah; and as they recounted the loss of someone famous and useful, they would bring to mind the loss sustained on account of him, and they would mourn. This became a tradition in Israel. It may have been that there was an annual remembrance of his death and the enormous loss it entailed.

We may gather much profit from considering the text, but there is one thing in particular that we may take as a foundation for several other lessons. It is that much honor, glory, and praise is due to a king because of his high office, but a double portion of such tribute is due to a good, gentle, virtuous Christian king.

David held Saul in high esteem because he was the anointed

of the Lord. He saved Saul's life, although Saul was seeking to take his life, and that because he was the anointed of the Lord. David killed the man who claimed to have killed Saul because he had killed the anointed of the Lord. David mourned for Saul as the anointed of the Lord. Jeremiah paid the greatest respect to Zedekiah and called him "the anointed of the Lord," "the breath of our nostrils," the "shadow" of Israel, even though Jeremiah had suffered under his rule and at his hand. The apostle Paul spoke with reverence of the Roman emperor and his officers, saying that their authority was from God and ordained by Him, that princes are the ministers and servants of God, and that those who oppose them will be judged. If Saul, Zedekiah, and Caesar received such honor from such notable men as David, Jeremiah, and Paul, what kind of honor and glory ought a Christian king, defender of religion and freedom of conscience, receive from his subjects? The names that are given to kings in the Word of God, and the manner in which their greatness and usefulness are expressed, reveal the honor and obedience that are their due.

1. The king is called the head of the nation. Saul was the head of the tribes of Israel and God made David the head of the heathen. The nation is compared to the body of a man and the rulers to the head. Isaiah speaks of the condition of the nation "from the sole of the foot even unto the head" (Isa. 1:6). The body is governed by the head, and if the members were to rise against the head, the result would be complete chaos.

2. The king is called he that rules over men. He is to sit on a throne and hold a scepter. The king is a governor under God, the King of all the earth, to rule over that portion of mankind entrusted to him by God. Paul says to the Romans that to rise up against him is to rebel against God.

3. Earthly kings and rulers are called gods. "I have said, Ye are gods ...but ye shall die like men." Kings bear the image of God as the Ruler of men. In terms of His holiness and goodness, God stamps

his image on the Christian, but in terms of His authority over the world He stamps His image on kings.

4. Kings are called the beauty of the nation. David weeps over Saul and Jonathan as the "beauty of Israel." A wise, gentle, good, and virtuous king is especially so.

5. A good king is called the light of the nation. David's men said that he should go out to battle with them no more lest he should quench "the light of Israel." Light is pleasant, comforting, and of great benefit. So is a virtuous king.

6. Jeremiah called Zedekiah "the breath of our nostrils." It is God who gives breath to all; it is He who gives a king to a nation and upholds him day by day. If the breath should depart without return-ing, that would be the end of all the operations of the body. So, when Zedekiah was taken away from Judah (and he was the last authentic king), like a body, it ceased to function.

7. A king is a shadow to a nation. Especially when he is a just and wise ruler he is "as the shadow of a great rock." It was said that the birds of the air and the beasts of the field found a dwelling and a shelter under the authority of Nebuchadnezzar. Some also found refuge in the power of Assyria. Much safer are the lives, posses-sions, privileges, and comforts of those ruled by a Christian king.

It is clear that honor and obedience are owing to kings, but consider the following truths:

1. God raises kings and grants kingdoms to whosoever He wills. This is said four times by Daniel in the fourth chapter of his prophecy, once by Nebuchadnezzar recounting his dream, once by Daniel interpreting the dream, and once by a voice from heaven ful-filling the dream. Kings are ordained by God and they are His ministers. It was He who gave, even to Nebuchadnezzar, kingdom, power, and glory. The customary manner in which God rules over the earth is through kings; He is the "Lord of kings." The Lord

Jesus Christ is the "King of kings" and "the Prince of the kings of the earth." "By me," says Christ, "kings reign." There will be kings in the most blessed period to be expected on earth. According to Isaiah, kings will be nursing fathers and queens nursing mothers to the church. Christ will be the King of kings while the earth lasts. That could never be if there were no kings on the earth.

2. It is God who, in His wrath, sets wicked kings over nations to punish them for their sins against Him. Sometimes He sets in authority over a nation the worst of men. One of the most severe of God's judgments is to set an evil king over it. God heard Israel complaining against Him and gave them Saul to be king over them in His indignation. God set Jehu as king over Israel to punish the sins of the house of Ahab, and Hazael over Syria to scourge them for their sins. God said of Israel through Hosea, "I gave thee a king in mine anger." Subjects ought to humble themselves for their own sins before God rather than complain and rebel if their rulers are ungodly and tyrannical. Rulers can be instruments to punish a nation, but it is the sins of the nation against God that are the root cause of all oppression and hardship. Sometimes kings are allowed to be influenced by wicked counsel, indeed, to yield to the incitement of Satan, to bring about the destruction of many of their subjects because of the wrath of the Lord against the nation on account of their sins. "And the anger of the Lord was kindled against Israel" (2 Kings 13:3). "And Satan…provoked David to number Israel" (1 Chron. 21:1). The hearts of kings are in the hand of the Lord—he can influence their thoughts and order their counsels however He chooses. It was because the Lord was angry with Judah and Jerusalem that Zedekiah rebelled against the king of Babylon, so that God could cast Judah out of His sight. Faced with all the foolish counsel and conduct of the rulers the nation should bow and repent, and seek reconciliation with the King of kings.

3. In His mercy to a nation and His love to His people within it, God sets a wise, virtuous king over it. In His mercy to Israel, God gave them David as king instead of Saul. "He brought him to feed

Jacob his people, and Israel his inheritance. So he fed them according to the integrity of his heart; and guided them by the skillfulness of his hands" (Ps. 78:71-72). One of God's greatest temporal mercies to a nation is a good and honorable king. "Blessed art thou, O land, when thy king is the son of nobles" (Eccl. 10:17).

A good king is a great benefit to a nation in civil and religious matters. His example is a blessing to the country in general; his wise counsel is a source of strength and shelter to his subjects, and his tenderness and gentleness a great comfort to all the nation. "He shall be as the light of the morning, when the sun rises, even a morning without clouds" (2 Sam. 23:4). It is a great help in matters of religion to be able to "lead a quiet and peaceable life in all godliness and honesty" (1 Tim. 2:2). To have a king who permits religious freedom is a great mercy, but to have a king who is himself religious and who defends religion is an even greater mercy. There are some kings today under whose authority there is no opportunity to live a godly life—and Britain has had many such in its history. But now it can be said, "The winter is past, the rain is over and gone; the flowers appear on the earth; the time of the singing of birds is come, and the voice of the turtle is heard in our land" (Song of Sol. 2:12). To have a wise, tender, godly head of a family is a great comfort and mercy to the family: but a nation is a far more numerous family, with the peace and comfort of thousands of other families depending on the peace and comfort of this vast family.

We see from what has been said that reverence and obedience are owing to a king as king, and doubly so to a good and virtuous king as long as he lives. We also have seen that mourning for him and esteem for his memory are fitting after his death.

Since this is so, those who disregard and disobey kings are guilty of great sin against God, and bring judgment on themselves, because they resist the ordinance of God. Those who despise authority see that the Bible is against them. Therefore, to confirm themselves in their erroneous and destructive opinions, and to make it easy for them to win more disciples to their way of thinking, they deny the inspiration of the Scriptures. Many of them deny the existence of God, and so give vent to their lusts in pursuing all manner of immorality and bloody cruelty. But God will soon make them aware, at their cost, of the fact that He does exist and that the Bible is divinely inspired. Let all who fear God and believe in the divinity of the Scriptures withdraw from them, and beware of their error, presumption, and blasphemy.

Furthermore, the removal of a good king through death is a cause of great grief to an entire nation, and it is our duty to pay due respect to such on his departure. By the death of a virtuous king a large family loses a kind father. Death climbs to the palaces, even to the highest court, and strikes the nation in its head, cuts down the excellence of the land, takes the light and hides it under the shadow of death, and makes orphans out of thousands upon thousands in one day. Oh, cruel death, the tears of a nation will not turn you away! In mourning a gentle king, remembering the misuse to which his quiet reign was put serves only to increase the grief. Again, in mourning, thanks ought to be given for the mercy that has been removed from us—thanks for the loan which is being returned. In this year, He who removes kings according to His wise and righteous ordering of events has placed our nation in a situation in which we all do well to grieve. He has taken from among us His Majesty George III, our most gracious king, whose reign was the best and longest of nearly all the kings of the world. If it were not for the fact that some things cause us to moderate our grief, it would be worthy to be compared to the mourning of Hadad-Rimmon, the mourning for the godly king Josiah. There are certain factors that charge us to restrain our grief, lest it become excessive.

1. We may celebrate his great age. He had reached the age of 81. Simply because of the design of God in setting a limit on the age of man, we could not have expected to keep him many more years.

2. We also recognize his infirmity and inability to be at the helm of government in the last nine years of his life. During this time he was unable to experience the distress or the consolation of the

nation. If, on the one hand, he was deprived of knowing the joy of the victory of Britain, and of knowing that the oppressor and disturber of Europe had been conquered and exiled, and that a general peace had been established, on the other hand he was kept from seeing the bitter troubles that afflicted his noble family. While he was in this unhappy condition, the young, beautiful, and honorable Princess Charlotte Augusta, accounted by some to be the hope of Britain, and her privileged baby were taken unexpectedly by death to eternity, without his feeling the pain as this close relationship was severed, and the desire of his eyes was taken away with a stroke. He did not hear the cry and mourning of the whole nation in this very sorrowful circumstance. Death came again and struck his royal partner, Queen Charlotte, the wife of his youth whom he loved as his own flesh. She was to him like "a loving hind and pleasant roe," and he was "ravished always with her love." Death broke the tie between them without his feeling any pain or concern. She was taken home without his shedding a tear. Death was allowed to march on and take his fourth son, the noble Prince Edward, Duke of Kent, the image of his father in so many virtues —temperate, serious, gentle, generous, and humble, patron and supporter of about twenty charitable societies. He himself was religious and respected any appearance of religion in all men, a sincere defender of the liberty of religion. For all his supremacy, his beauty and merits, he was cut down by death in the midst of his days. His death caused much grieving and many tears throughout the United Kingdom. This, however, passed without His Majesty feeling any care or grief, uttering no sigh, shedding no tear, not knowing that his dear Edward had preceded him, until he should meet him in the realm of spirits.

3. The pleasant memories we have of him as a Christian moderate our grief. It was better for him in death to be a Christian than to be the king of Great Britain with one ninth of the inhabitants of the earth under his authority. Death is such a benefit to the Christian, that it is no loss for a godly king to die, for it is far better to be with Christ.

4. Our hope that our present king, His Majesty George IV, will walk the same noble paths that his father walked also moderates our grief. Our hopes are confirmed as we consider his talents and fitness to rule over this great nation, and also from the proof we had during the nine years of his regency, and the effort he put into doing things the way he thought his father would have done. Chiefly, however, our hope is strengthened as we think of the goodness of the Lord to the nation in spite of its sinfulness, and that God has many people in the nation with a great work for them to do. He has chosen them to be instruments in His hand to spread the knowledge of Him through the whole world. Therefore we are confident that God will give freedom, quietness, and protection to us under the wing of the reign of our present king to carry on His great and glorious work without hindrance.

Further, I will note certain features, according to the little knowledge I have, of the manner, demeanor, virtue, and excellence of His Majesty our late king, George III. In some respects there is no doubt that there has never been his equal in Britain. There have been twenty kings in Britain from Egbert, the first Englishman to reign, until William the Conqueror, but not one of them had virtues to compare with George III, apart from King Alfred. There have been thirty-two kings since William to the present, but none of them like George III. It is true that Edward VI, and William and Mary were renowned for many reasons, but their reign was so short and the times so dark that it is not possible to compare them with George III. Queen Elizabeth had many outstanding features, but the suffering of thousands of godly people in her days is a cloud on her reputation and her good name as a Christian queen, even to the present day. It can truthfully be said that God in His mercy to this kingdom, and to His people in it, set the House of Brunswick on the throne of Britain. By a great effort the succession was settled on none but a Protestant ruler. In the reign of King William III, and before the end of the reign of Queen Anne, it was only a very little that turned the scales in favor of the House of Brunswick.

Nevertheless, He in whose power it lies to raise kings ordained that this family should inherit the throne in order that they should foster the church in this island, and that they should be patrons of the spread of the gospel all over the world. Britain was never so happy as it has been since the ascent of this family to the throne, and the cause of Christ has never enjoyed so much peace on our island nor so much protection from the throne, as it has under the rule of this gentle family.

In the following observations it is evident that it is not too much to say that there never was in Britain his equal as a king in all manner of virtues.

1. Primarily, his sobriety and religious tendency were exceptional from his youth. When he was very young, he was put in the charge of Dr. Ayscough, afterwards Dean of Bristol, who testified of his remarkable inclinations and his delight in matters of religion. When he was six years old he learned, without any persuasion from others, some excerpts from Philip Doddridge's work on the principles of Christianity. There is reason to believe that his parents, Frederick and Augusta, Prince and Princess of Wales, held morality and true religion in high esteem. Frederick died when his son, the future king, was twelve years old. Princess Augusta was very careful to bring up her children with moral standards. She said that she was afraid of the influence of the young nobility of that age on Prince George because of the bad examples they set. On another occasion she said that nothing mattered to her so much as to see him succeed and make the nation happy—a wish that was granted.

2. Furthermore, when George II died suddenly and the news was broken to the prince that he was now to be king, he answered the challenge like a man, indeed, like a Christian conscious of his utter inability to occupy such an exalted position. Nonetheless, he would make it his life's work to further in every respect the happiness of the kingdom and to defend and confirm its religious and national establishments.

His first appearance among the people as king pleased them

very much. One of his first actions was to issue a proclamation throughout the kingdom against wickedness, immorality, profaning the Sabbath, and other evils. This declaration is still to be read in every Quarter Session, in every church, and in the chapels associated with the Established Church every three months. His Majesty said that throughout his reign he would give every encouragement to those who were religious and set himself against those who were irreligious.

His demeanor on the day of his coronation was commendable and truly Christian. As he approached the Lord's Table after he was crowned, he took off his crown, put it to one side, and said to the Archbishop that he would not approach the King of kings with his crown on his head. He insisted that the queen do the same thing. She responded that her dress would be disordered, and that she would therefore be ridiculed. He said that if it were so, let the crown be counted part of her clothing while she received the ordinance. His Majesty laid aside his crown on the day he received it, before the "prince of the kings of the earth," on whose head are many crowns. We may well believe that it will be his work for ever to cast his crown at His feet. He wore his earthly crown long after he laid it before the "King of kings," but after placing the crown before the Lord Jesus, and acknowledging that his salvation was entirely of Him, he shall wear the incorruptible crown forever.

3. Furthermore, Britain loved him because his tender care for his subjects was exceptional. He was in truth the father of his people. He showed genuine heart concern for their temporal and eternal happiness. For their sakes, as well as in fulfillment of the requirements of his high office, so great was his concern for keeping the laws and form of the government from being corrupted that one nobleman often said that the king would live on bread and water to preserve the form of government of the land, and that he would give his life to keep her from harm. After he ascended the throne the Bishop of London greeted him with these words, "You, sir, are the one the people desire. By declaring your concern for their prosperity, you are returning the affection they have for you. Let there

be only one matter for debate. Whose is the greater love, the king's for the people or the people's for the king? And let it be a long debate, continuing indefinitely, without arriving at a conclusion, but with the result always undecided. Let there be fatherly affection on one side and filial obedience on the other, with enduring remembrance of both. May the God of heaven and earth keep you always under His protection and lead you to seek His honor and glory in all that you do, so that you may reap the reward by your increase in happiness in this world and in that which is to come." The wishes of the bishop were to a large degree answered. It was difficult to know who loved whom the more, the king or the people. He showed great love for them while he retained his senses, and his subjects displayed the greatest affection for him in their esteem and obedience, thousands of prayers being offered on his behalf at all times. It is likely that the Lord heard His people's prayers for him, and answered them by restoring him on one occasion from his sickness and infirmity. It is likely that God had a beneficial purpose in his restoration at that time, for there were many grand accomplishments in his reign towards the end of his life.

Several charitable societies were established; religious freedom was secured, and before his death, peace was restored to a large part of the world. He occupied a large place in the affections of his subjects until he died. Indeed, I can say all his subjects. The few who did not respect him were not worthy of the name Britons, and they themselves reject the name of Christians. They are the refuse of the people and the scum of the nation.

People of every degree, among them the wisest and best of religious men in the kingdom, respected George III. In him the affection of the entire nation found an object as a focal point. As a result of loving him, many learned to love one another. Some kings in Britain were revered greatly by a few of their subjects and by some religious party in the kingdom, but another party would find complaint against them and find fault in them. If the nobles were being pleased, the common people would murmur that they were being ignored and oppressed. If churchmen were being pleased, the

nonconformists would lament because of their distress and persecution. If the nonconformists were being favored by the throne, the
churchmen would be loud in their outcry that the church was in
danger and the king bereft of any zeal for her. In George III, however, men of every degree, party, and name were content. His
exemplary, gentle, cheerful manner pleased the great ones at court;
and his humility, kindness, and tenderness rejoiced the hearts of all
the common people in the land. He had great respect for the Established Church, and was scrupulous in his attendance at its services.
There was nothing cold about his worship; his Christian attitude
was a tribute to the church, and delighted every ordinary church-
man throughout the kingdom.

In his answer to an address by the people called the Quakers
soon after he ascended the throne, he revealed his principle and
intention relating to religious liberty. It was according to his promise at that time that he acted throughout his long reign. He declared
that he was absolutely determined to preserve religious liberty without fear or favor, and that the civil and religious rights of his
subjects were dear to him, and the most valuable of the privileges
of his crown. He could not bear the thought of restricting freedom.
If anyone sought to lead him along that path he would dismiss
them with one word: "No religious persecution in my days!" He
happened on one occasion to pass through a little town near one of
his palaces when the inhabitants of the town had risen against a
few nonconformists who had come there to worship. His Majesty
commanded his chariot to stop and demanded to know the reason
for the disturbance. On being told, he said that the people who were
being persecuted were good, harmless, and did not intend evil to
anybody. It was better for the people of the town to leave them
alone. If anyone under his authority should hound them, those
people would themselves immediately be punished. That was
enough to end that outburst.

Once, on returning to his palace, he came across a religious
maid in his household in tears. He questioned her carefully and discovered that one of the maids senior to her had prevented her from

going to hear a preacher who was in the neighborhood that day. The king called that maid to him and rebuked her sharply, adding, "There will be no religious persecution during my reign."

His Majesty was fond of giving employment for those who were religious, making no distinction between churchmen and nonconformists. Often on a Monday morning he took delight in inquiring where they had been on the Sabbath, whom they had heard, what was the text, and sometimes about the heads of the sermon. On occasion, he would ask the nonconformists whether their minister prayed for him, and when told that they did, he was highly pleased.

Although His Majesty was intensely concerned about liberty of religion, there were some who held office under him who were guilty of persecution. This was a cause of grief to him. We see evidence of this in the following account. When His Majesty was repairing his palace at Kew, one of the workers was a godly man of a tender conscience. The king loved to converse with him about important matters. One Monday morning, His Majesty went to look for the workman according to his custom, but could not find him. He made enquiries and some of the other workers who were over the man had to confess that they had been completing some task that they had on the Sabbath morning. The other workman had refused to work with them, and for that reason they had turned him away from his work. "Send for him at once," said His Majesty. "The man who refuses to work on the Lord's Day is the man for me. Send for him." The king showed favor to him from then on. On a similar occasion he said, "I am the defender of the faith, and yet I do not allow a man to be dismissed because of his religion!"

4. The way in which he conducted himself in the family was exemplary. One man said, "His Majesty had a family as well as a throne; he was a husband and father as well as a prince." His exceptional character as a man devoted to his family won the applause of his people, and the love of his family. He was known for the value he set on God's mercies. He would get up early each morning and spend an hour in his room reading the Word of God and praying. In eating and drinking it can be said that he was "the son of

nobles," one of those princes "who eat in due season, for strength, and not for drunkenness."

He was affectionate and faithful to his life's partner, tender as a father, and very careful to bring up his children "in the nurture and admonition of the Lord," as was testified by one of his sons now reunited to his father by death (Eph. 6:4). This was also borne out by the loving and serious way he spoke of Christ, and the way of reconciliation through His blood at the deathbed of the lovely Princess Amelia. It was further confirmed by the testimony of the worthy, beautiful, late Princess Charlotte, who said with tears as she spoke, that her grandfather had often said to her that nothing would smooth the bed of death but true faith in Christ and being under the influences of the Holy Spirit.

5. The worship and ordinances of the house of God were highly esteemed by His Majesty, and he was careful to sanctify the Sabbath. He was scorned for being so scrupulous in this by the irreligious, but let us pray that his splendid example be followed by the great ones in Britain. Someone said, "Let the command of God be heard from the grave of our king, 'Remember the Sabbath day, to keep it holy.'"

He had a high regard for evangelical books and sermons. It is said that one godly minister who had been appointed to preach before the king had mistakenly brought with him a sermon different from the one he had intended to bring. Because of this he was compelled to preach before His Majesty a sermon composed to be preached in a clear evangelical fashion to his poor parishioners. After the sermon the king came to greet him very warmly. The preacher began to apologize, saying that he was afraid that he had displeased His Majesty by preaching in such a way before him; that it was by mistake that he had brought that sermon which had been prepared for the poor members of his flock. "Well," said His Majesty, "whenever you come here to preach again, be sure to bring one of the sermons preached to your poor people—that is the kind of sermon that suits me."

While preaching before His Majesty, one minister mentioned

some words by a certain author concerning self-control. The king asked him who the author was. The minister replied that it was a Baptist minister in Yorkshire. His Majesty obtained the book and read it with great delight. Later he sent to the author to acknowledge the pleasure he had derived from reading the book, and to express his wish to help him in whatever way he thought best. The minister, Mr. Fawcett (later Dr. Fawcett) thanked the king for the favor and honor bestowed on him, but declined from asking a favor at that time. Some time after, a friend of Mr. Fawcett's found himself in distress because his son had been found guilty of forgery, a capital offence. Mr. Fawcett wrote to the king to plead for the young man's life. His wish was granted, to the surprise of all who knew the circumstances. I give this summary of the account to show the delight His Majesty had taken in this good book, and how gracious and tender he was in his attitude to the author.

6. Apart from the things already recounted, His Majesty possessed many other conspicuous virtues impossible to mention. It was remarkable how he discerned the hand of the Lord in various instances. When an attempt was made on his life by someone shooting through the window of his carriage, he turned to his nobles who were attending him in great fear. "Well, my lords," he said, "One proposes one thing and another something else, and they forget that there is One over us all, who rules over all things, and it is upon Him alone that we depend."

His Majesty loved to show forgiveness and would not allow the taking of the life of those who sought his own. He was also exceptionally generous; many examples of this characteristic could be given. It is said that he made annual donations of £14,000 to various good causes.

7. The country experienced much prosperity in national, moral, and religious matters in his days. I will not speak at length of national affairs, such as the extending of the boundaries of the kingdom and the notable victories. There was growth in such fields as education and knowledge of the arts. Trade, labor, communities,

and families all drew benefit from his reign. However, greater joy and comfort are to be found in considering the success that attended morality and religion while he was on the throne. It could be said of him as of King Solomon, "Thus Solomon finished the house of the LORD, and the king's house: and all that came into Solomon's heart to make in the house of the LORD, and in his own house, he prosperously effected" (2 Chron. 7:11). The Lord prospered his cause, honored the gospel marvelously while he was king, not only in Britain, but also, by the labor of God's people in Britain, through many parts of the world.

The work that God accomplished in Wales during His Majesty's reign was astonishing. If we were to compare the condition of this country now with its state before George III ascended the throne, what reason would we have to cry out with wonder, "What hath God wrought!" Many thousands of the subjects of George III, called by grace in his days, went to heaven before him. It is very unlikely that any king who has gone to heaven since the beginning of the world, has seen as many of his subjects there before him as George III.

If in years to come someone should ask, "When did many well-known and charitable societies and associations begin," the answer will have to be, "In the days of George III." When were the oppressed children of Africa released, and when did Britain wash her hands of the bloody slave trade? When was the Sunday School movement established, and many missionary societies? When was that excellent organization, the Bible Society, established? And when was religious freedom secured and extended? Answer: In the reign of George III. The societies named above execute the wishes of His Majesty, who said that he wished that every child in his kingdom could read the Bible.

His Majesty recommended and encouraged the way in which many parents brought their children up to know the Bible. One day, on seeing the work of one Mr. West who had drawn representations of scenes from the Bible, a bishop who was present remarked that this was a proof that Mr. West was very well acquainted with the Bible. The king asked the bishop whether he knew how this had come about. The bishop replied that he did not. "I will tell you, my lord," said the king, "Mr. West's parents were Quakers, and they teach their children to read the Bible while they are very young. I wish it were more like that with us, my lord."

His Majesty used to recover his senses for a few moments sometimes in his last illness, but not very often. On hearing the clock at Windsor strike one day he asked who had died. The reply came that it was a Mrs. S-. His Majesty then mentioned the name of the street where she lived, and added, "She was a good woman, and brought up her family to fear God. She has gone to heaven. I hope I shall follow her soon." By this we see that the things of God and of heaven were on his mind even in his sad condition.

It is said that the queen was told that he had such lucid moments, and that she desired to know the next time there would be an indication of this. She was informed. She went in and found him singing a hymn. Then he fell to his knees and prayed aloud— for Her Majesty, then for his family and the nation. He ended by praying for himself, if God would be pleased to take away his heavy burden. If not, that he would enable him to bear it.

Now all his distress is over, and the long period of his peaceable reign has come to an end. In speaking of his virtues I am aware that God in His mercy and goodness gave them all, and that God is worthy of all the praise—and He shall have it. While he lived, George III could not endure to be praised. Certainly he desires none now. "Not unto us," is the language of the world where he now is.

I would like to draw your attention to some lessons in closing.

1. We see that the most precious and delightful temporal mercies are only for a little while. Britain had George III for a long time, but now that time has come to a close, and God has taken the loan home. We give thanks for the virtues that were found in him, and the quietness and privileges we enjoyed under his rule, and we grieve because we did not make better use of them.

2. We see that no earthly greatness preserves us from death. Although the psalmist calls kings and princes gods, they die like men—and many of them die the most horrible death. Out of sixty-three Roman emperors, only six of them died a natural death. It is a mercy to a land that its king goes to the grave in peace. How fragile is the most sublime greatness of the world! It will not keep death at bay, but the greatest will be the equal of the weakest in the grave.

3. Death is no loss to the godly man, no matter how exalted his position, or how comfortable his lot in the world. To be with Christ is far better. It is not in the world that the home of the godly is to be found, but in a better land. Let us ask ourselves when death comes, Will it be loss or gain for us when it comes? Dying is of such great consequence that it is bound to be the greatest loss or gain for us.

4. God is the eternal and immortal King. Christ, the King over Zion, lives for ever. He will rule over the house of Jacob and of His kingdom there shall be no end. It cannot be said of Zion, "There arose up a new king…which knew not Joseph" (Ex. 1:8). Although death cuts down the kings of the earth one after the other, the Prince of the kings of the earth lives, and He will live eternally. Zion will never again wear her garments of mourning for her king.

Although Britain has lost George III, He who gave him to her is yet alive, and His strength as great as ever, and His treasure as abundant as ever. He can adorn his son with the same virtues as the father. Let us pray for him always, so that the King of kings will lead, defend, and uphold His Majesty George IV, that it may be said that he walked in all the virtuous ways of his father. Let us honor him, and let us pray constantly for him—but let us trust in the Lord who rules in the kingdom of men. And since "The LORD reigneth; let the earth rejoice; let the multitude of isles be glad thereof" (Ps. 97:1). Let us rejoice, also, island of Britain, for He is our God. Amen.

The Coming of the Son of Man

"Behold, I come as a thief. Blessed is he that watcheth, and keep-
eth his garments, lest he walk naked, and they see his shame."
—Revelation 16:15

In this chapter, we have portrayed the seven angels pouring out the seven last plagues, which were to be poured upon the enemies of the church of Christ on earth. They were all to fall on the ungodly, and it was the destruction of the ungodly that was their purpose, especially those who were particularly hostile and viciously opposed to the church and cause of God.

In the vision, it is the angels who are said to send the plagues on the earth, although it is men who are chiefly the agents employed. This is to show God's judgments are executed through His messengers, whosoever He chooses to use in the execution of His will. Furthermore, though they may be unaware of it, His purpose is being realized through them.

The first verse in the chapter reads, "And I heard a great voice out of the temple saying to the seven angels, Go your ways, and pour out the vials of the wrath of God upon the earth." The word "vials" is used mainly to show that the judgments of God are according to measure. Some divines consider that only one of the vials has been poured out as yet, and that the other six are yet to come. Others say that five, and others six, have already been emptied. I humbly submit that five have already been outpoured, and the sixth in part, or is being poured out at present. These words in our text, I believe, refer to the sixth vial. Therefore I shall look for a little while at this sixth vial before coming to the text.

In verse twelve we read, "And the sixth angel poured out his vial upon the great river Euphrates; and the water thereof was dried up, that the way of the kings of the east might be prepared." The mighty Euphrates was then a source of strength and power to the city of Babylon, and a secure defense on that side against any attack. It was one of the chief obstacles preventing any enemy from taking the city.

The errors that were to come on the earth, especially the kingdom of the beast, or popery, are often in this book indicated by the name "Babylon." There is a perfect fitness in the name, because as Babylon and the Babylonians were the great enemies of the people and Israel of God, so Roman Catholicism in every age has been the enemy of the church of God. She is so filled with blood and the filth of idolatry and every unclean thing, that she is well named "Babylon the great, the mother of harlots and abominations of the earth." And whatever is meant by "Euphrates," it is evident that it is something which gives power to Babylon or Catholicism.

Some are of the opinion that Euphrates here refers to the Turk and the Mohammedan religion, since these are a support and defense to Catholicism, so much so that the one cannot be subdued while the other is in authority. But when the water of this river is dried up through the complete disappearance of the empire of the Turks and Islam has perished from the earth, then the obstacle will be removed and the way made clear for the destruction of the spiritual Babylon, and the abolition of Romanism from the face of the earth.

But I fail to see that this is all that is implied here. Rather, I tend to think that the river Euphrates refers not only to the things mentioned but along with them to all the treasure and powers of the kingdoms which defend and sustain the popish religion. They are the source of the wealth and pomp, luxury and pride of the church of Rome, and the chief means of her support. Also, the drying of the river means her impoverishment and her deprivation of the riches and defense afforded by these kingdoms. When the church of Rome loses her wealth and greatness, and God weakens and reduces her through turning away or drying up the stream of her possessions and support, then she will sink to nothingness and die of herself as a consequence. In this sense she has already dried to a large extent because of the changes that have lately occurred. She is far less wealthy now than she used to be, and far less distinguished in the eyes of the kings of the earth. Traces of the drying up of the river are already visible, as well as the restriction of the supply of her water.

The consequence of this is said to be "that the way of the kings of the east might be prepared." According to some, this means the calling of the Jews, or the turning of the Jewish nation to Christianity. As the subjugation of Babylon formerly was the means of the liberation of the Jews from captivity, so the subjection of the spiritual Babel will be the occasion of their freedom from the captivity of unbelief. I have nothing against this interpretation so far as it goes, but I think the words have a wider application. Although I do not by any means rule out the above explanation, I think the reference to the kings of the east is to be taken literally. The kings or emperors of China, Burma, Siam, and Japan will welcome the Bible and receive the gospel in their empires, where now Romanism is a hindrance and an obstacle to the acceptance of Christianity. Then the ministers of the word will have free access beyond their borders to proclaim the gospel of Christ throughout those dark, wide, and populous regions, and so through the entire world.

The following verses read, "And I saw three unclean spirits like frogs come out of the mouth of the dragon, and out of the mouth of the beast, and out of the mouth of the false prophet. For they are the spirits of devils, working miracles, which go forth unto the kings of the earth and of the whole world, to gather them to the battle of that great day of God Almighty" (Rev. 16:13-14).

These three spirits of devils are called three unclean spirits on account of their number, and to indicate the three sources of error from which they issued—the dragon, the beast, and the false prophet. They were like frogs; that is, they had the appearance of monsters. I think that the spirit coming out of the mouth of the dragon represents the infidelity of this age, modern paganism. The spirit from the mouth of the beast represents the errors encouraged by tyrants who support and are in alliance with the beast, together with everything that is opposed to the truth. The false prophet stands not only for Mohammedanism, but also for the oppressive rule of the pope, all the ecclesiastical dominion of the Antichrist. It stands for the oppressive authority of Islam and Catholicism.

By "the spirits of devils," we are to understand not only the evil spirits or the devils themselves, but also men under the control of an evil spirit. They are men with the spirit of devils and completely under their authority. They are natural, carnal, cunning men, professing themselves to have spiritual motives but really with nothing of the kind, like the Jesuits and Catholic missionaries whose task is to employ every device to oppose and withhold the light of the gospel. As has already been said, they are compared to frogs, and the comparison between them is very suggestive.

They are like frogs because they are nurtured in dirty, muddy waters; that is, they are nurtured in the doctrines of devils. Like frogs they make the most sound in the darkness. They are so afraid of the light that even the flicker of a candle reduces the level of the noise they make, and the light of the sun silences them completely. So it is with these spiritual frogs. The darkness of ignorance and error is their strength, but they will not stand for a moment before the light of the gospel. They become quiet and they die like the frogs of Egypt before the powerful light of the Sun of Righteousness. Again, they are like frogs in that they are able to live in water and on land. Indeed, these are frogs the like of which have never been seen, able to live in water and in fire, wherever darkness rules. It is said that these spirits can work miracles; that is, they appear to work miracles so that they can enchant more and be more successful in deceiving.

The "kings of the earth" here means the pagan princes and principalities, which are supportive of and favorable to Antichrist. And "the whole world" stands for as many of the nations of the world as they can take with them. The purpose is to gather them for war, an assault on the kingdom of Christ and all the saints of the Most High. The place where they will be gathered together is called Armageddon.

The occasion when all these things will be fulfilled is called "the great day of God Almighty." This is one of those great and terrible days of the Lord. The only one I shall name at present is the day of the fall of Jerusalem and the dispersion of the Jewish nation. Never was there distress on the face of the earth like this, the tribulation that overtook the Jews in the war with the Romans, when the city was besieged by the Roman forces under Titus Vespasian. There was greater anguish and distress in Jerusalem on that day than there had ever been in any battle in the Valley of Megiddo.

So we come to the text. It is as though God was saying that there is another great and terrible day to come. This is how it will come, and blessed will be those who are prepared. There are two things that are set out.

I. The Son of Man will come, and He will come "as a thief"
II. The attitude of those who are ready, or a description of the blessed man: "Blessed is he that watcheth, and keepeth his garments, lest he walk naked, and they see his shame"

I. Nothing is more certain than that He will come, and the Lord here warns those who expect Him, how unexpected that coming will be. It is when men are in a deep sleep, and midway through the night that the thief usually comes. So will the coming of the Son of Man be. Following are some of the features of that event.

First, like a thief, He will be unexpected. "If the good man of the house had known in what watch the thief would come, he would have watched, and would not have suffered his house to be broken up" (Matt. 24:43). "If therefore thou shalt not watch, I will come on thee as a thief, and thou shalt not know what hour I will come upon thee" (Rev. 3:3).

Second, He will come as a thief because He will come when men are asleep. "The day of the Lord so cometh as a thief in the night.... But ye, brethren, are not in darkness, that that day should overtake you as a thief.... Therefore let us not sleep, as do others; but let us watch and be sober" (1 Thess. 5).

Third, He will come when men are not ready. That day will take everyone unawares except for those who are found watching. "Be ye therefore ready also" (Luke 12:40).

And finally, as when a thief comes, many will sustain a great loss and will be robbed of what they possess when He comes. They will be robbed of their empty hope, of the advantages that they mis-used, and of the privileges that they despised. Those who are caught unprepared by that day will be kept poor indeed. "Blessed is he that watcheth, and keepeth his garments, lest he walk naked, and they see his shame" (Rev. 16:15).

II. Whatever distress there will be on earth in those days, and how-ever terrifying will be the fate of the world, yet there is a way to be happy, even then. The Lord is able to save the righteous *from* trou-ble, *in* trouble, and *out* of trouble, and is able to make him and his own very happy even in the midst of the greatest dangers. The words of the text are the shout of the Lord over His beloved ones and the sound of the trumpet of God to His people. This blessed man is described in two ways:

1. He keeps his garments
2. He watches

1. The blessed man keeps his garments. This saying is used in one of two ways that were familiar to the Jews of those days. It might be taken from a military custom among the Romans. If a Roman soldier was found sleeping on his watch, and if for this offence his life was spared, he would be stripped of his uniform and thus appear naked and be dismissed in disgrace. Or it might refer to another well-known occurrence relating to the service of the tem-ple. According to historians, there was one official of the temple whose duty it was to stand on his feet all night, and to walk about as a watchman at different intervals with a lighted torch to see whether the priests and Levites were awake and about their tasks. If he found anyone asleep during his watch in the temple of God,

that man's garments would be burned, and the following morning he would be compelled to appear in his charred clothing. This also was accounted a great disgrace. For this reason it was right and proper to warn those who had kept themselves until that time to be careful to keep their garments so that they might complete their course with their reputations untarnished. Let us pray that if the Lord decides to pour out His judgment on the nations, He will in mercy send watchmen to arouse His people before He comes.

2. The blessed man is portrayed as one who watches. I must remind you of the danger of not watching, the great profit of watching, and the duty and obligation of every Christian to watch.

The danger of not watching is that we shall suffer great loss. We shall lose the sweet presence of God, and the assurance of our relationship with Him. Along with this, we shall lose our usefulness in His service and much of our happiness along the way. There are great consequences to failing to watch. However, if we do watch, there is immense profit. The one who watches keeps on the right way; he beautifies his profession, and he preserves his garments and his profession. All the benefits spoken of in the text are his— he will have heaven on the way to heaven and he will have great gain. There is infinite worth in watching.

Every Christian has an obligation to watch. The duty of watching is frequently urged upon people in the Bible. "What," asks Christ of His disciples in the garden when He found them sleeping, "could ye not watch with me one hour?" (Matt. 26:40). The duty of watching is presented to us in three ways in the Bible: watching as opposed to sleep, watching as opposed to idleness, and watching as opposed to carelessness and indifference regarding the coming of the Lord.

a. *Watching as opposed to sleeping.* This contrast is frequently set out in the Bible; for example, "Awake thou that sleepest, and arise from the dead, and Christ shall give thee light" (Eph. 5:14). Do not be like those who are dead, for when we are asleep we are as though we were dead and completely incapable of watching. When a man is asleep, his senses are locked up, his limbs useless, and his whole body idle. When a Christian goes to sleep, he is good for nothing; his spiritual senses are imprisoned, all his graces are idle, and he is sunk in lethargy. But when he is awake and watchful, he is very different. His senses are lively, his members are industrious, his graces are gleaming and fruitful. He looks to see where danger lies and he is motivated by the spirit of doing good. While the Christian's graces are astir, his attitude will be lively and alert. He will long to benefit his fellow creatures, and be eager and careful for the glory of God in the world.

b. *Watching as opposed to idleness and laziness.* "Be ye steadfast, unmovable, always abounding in the work of the Lord, forasmuch as ye know that your labor is not in vain in the Lord" (1 Cor. 15:58). "Blessed is he that watcheth," that is, not idle and lazy, but vigilant, awake, and industrious in the cause of the Lord.

c. *Watching as opposed to being thoughtless and indifferent regarding the coming of the Lord.* The man who watches is looking for the day of the coming of the Lord, and for "the glorious appearing of the great God and our Saviour Jesus Christ." I fear that there is precious little of this looking in the world at present, indeed, much less than in days gone by. There must be a powerful reason to account for such a change as this. Either God has altered the form of religion or else there is now barely a trace of it in the world. This was the kind of religion that characterized primitive Christianity, looking for the coming of the Lord, "having a desire to depart, and to be with Christ" (Phil. 1:23). The early Christians were like servants expecting their Lord, however and whenever He chose to come, saying, "Come, Lord, in whichever way and at whatever time Thou wilt, because we are waiting for Thee, and our souls are at peace with Thee."

There are three reasons why a Christian should watch. First, he must watch out of concern for his own safety, then for his usefulness, and finally for his present happiness, although his eternal happiness does not depend on this.

We must watch for the sake of our safety. On our pilgrimage there are many enemies—the wiles of Satan, the great deceitfulness of the heart, the snares that are in our way, all revealing the need to watch and to be extremely vigilant. Failure to be watchful has brought the most serious and bitter consequences to the saints. What are these consequences? They vary: Samson lost his eyes; David his peace; Peter his comfort, and Noah, Moses, and others suffered immense loss through lack of watchfulness. If the righteous sleeps on the knees of some Delilah, he will lose his hair, his strength, his eyes, as well as his comfort and usefulness, and will know an indescribable bitterness. Watch, therefore, and pray that you do not fall into temptation.

Secondly, we need to watch for the sake of our usefulness. Unless we watch we will lose our usefulness, our crown, our respect, our strength, our honor, and our value for the work and cause of God. We will lose our position in God's house and with His people. For this reason, brethren, watch, so that you preserve your usefulness.

Thirdly, we must watch out of concern for our present happiness, and our delight and comfort on our journey. If we do not watch we shall experience only discomfort, tribulation, and care on the earth, and shall meet death under a cloud. There will be terror in the valley, and darkness and fear in the river. How hard it will be for you when you die, and how heavy it will be for you in the river if you go there without a watchful spirit. Like a disobedient child you will have to go to bed without a candle. You will have to face the next world without knowing where you are going and without leaving any testimony to your brothers after you. Those who loved you will be forced to say with much anxiety after your departure, "This man has left us, but we do not know where he has gone. He has died and we do not know whether heaven or hell is his home. What makes our grief more bitter than anything is that he was in a thick mist in the valley, in an impenetrable darkness before going into the river, and there we left him and lost him. We heard him going into the water, but for all the world we could not say whether he landed on the other side. We have no evidence of his state because of the darkness that surrounded him and us." The happiness of the Christian in his life and death, his strong consolation in living and dying, is a pearl without price, and reason enough for us all to be careful that we do not lose it.

There are many other things we could mention, if we had time, that call us urgently to watch. The day is short; the task is immense; the judgment is meticulous and near; the snares are frequent on the way; the enemies are many and powerful. We need to guard against the plague of the deceitfulness of the heart, the snares and devices and cunning of the devil, that we may be safe from all evil.

In closing, let me briefly refer to the last part of the text. He keeps his garments in two ways: from being plundered, and from being contaminated. The words obviously imply that he has garments; otherwise, they could not be spoiled. In that day the King will say to many who deceived the eyes of the watchers, "Friend, how camest thou in hither not having a wedding garment?" (Matt. 22:12). By this "wedding garment," the King means the image of God, the righteousness of Christ, all the influences of His Spirit, and a life consistent with the gospel.

The blessed man has garments, and here they are: he has the righteousness of Christ about him; he has put on the new man; he has put on the Lord Jesus Christ, together with bowels of mercies and love, as the elect of God.

The blessed man has kept them so that he was not robbed of them. He was attentive to his profession and his livery. He did not lose his military uniform by displeasing his King. Christian, see that you do not offend God in case you lose the honor of owning the Lord Jesus Christ on earth and standing for Him in the world. Blessed is the man who keeps his garments from being stolen. Who is he? He is the one who cleaves to the Lord until the last, serves Him with a devoted heart, keeps the faith, adorns his profession, and ploughs his furrow to the end. This is the one who carries the banner to the finish, keeps his livery to the hour of death, has his military uniform about him in the waters, keeps his profession, remains with Jesus and the battle until its close, and stands a faithful soldier all the way. This is the man of whom it is said, "Blessed is he." And he will be blessed.

Furthermore, he keeps his garments and profession from being tainted with sin, from being marred by the spirit of the world, from immorality, backsliding, a declining spirit, and distancing his soul from God. Blessed is such a man!

What does it mean to walk naked? It means to walk without a profession, or, in spite of having a profession to walk without adorning it, and to live a life which does not conform to the gospel of Christ. It is to live without making a public avowal of the Lord, without the shelter of God and the defense of the Almighty. It is said that Israel was naked when God had withdrawn Himself from her. Only dishonor awaits a Christian without his profession, because apart from this, he is without even the appearance of godliness and walks in a backslidden way.

When men walk naked their shame is exposed. When Jesus comes to judge men, how ugly and hideous will backsliders and hypocrites seem! So will it be with men having no power of godliness, just like Samson and Peter when they went to the enemy's territory. What a disgrace for Samson, the champion of Israel, when the Philistines had put out his eyes! How unsightly and odious did Peter look in the court of the high priest, denying his Lord and Redeemer, swearing and cursing before his Master's enemies, insisting that he did not know the man! We are in danger of falling into the same shame unless we watch. Therefore, brethren, let us watch. Listen to the warning in the text. Hear the cry of the Lord to His beloved ones, and the sound of the trumpet of God to His people to rouse them to vigilance before His coming in judgment. Nothing is more certain than His coming, although we do not know when that will be. Even if you do not meet with any of God's fearful visitations or temporal judgments yet you will meet with death! This will be exactly the same, and that sooner, while the last judgment will be later. No one escapes death or avoids the judgment. We shall all be brought to death without exception and we shall all appear in the dreaded judgment. Therefore, let us be sure we are saved, let us be reconciled to God, and let all come to see His salvation who as yet have not done so.

Oh, God, awaken sleepers, give life to those who are dead, for our benefit and Thy glory. Amen.

Christ the Physician

*"Is there no balm in Gilead; is there no physician there? Why then
is not the health of the daughter of my people recovered?"*
—Jeremiah 8:22

It is very sobering to think of a man dying within reach of the
means of saving him, or to see a dying man refusing medicine
because he is angry with the doctor. Although men do not normally
behave in this way, this is the attitude of thousands in a spiritual
sense to the salvation of God—the balm. The balm of Gilead was
a kind of liquid or valuable juice which dripped from some trees in
Gilead under the influence of the heat of the sun. There were many
of these trees growing on the hills of Gilead, and the fierce heat of
the sun drew out this precious liquid, which had exceptionally
effective healing properties. In the hands of skilled physicians, this
balm was an almost infallible cure for all kinds of ailments. In this
region lived many skilled and experienced doctors to prepare this
medicine, and it was unusual to hear of anyone dying from sickness
in the vicinity. The prophet uses this as an illustration of the spiritual condition of men in the land of religious privileges and
benefits, and the text is a reference to this: "Is there no balm in
Gilead; is there no physician there? Why then is not the health of
the daughter of my people recovered?"

Three questions are asked in these words, and the third is
asked on the understanding that the first two have been answered
in the affirmative. "Is there no balm in Gilead?" "Yes." "Is there no
physician there?" "Yes." "Why then is not the health of the daughter of my people recovered?" If the first two were answered in the
negative, there would be no need to ask the third. The inquirer

would then naturally say that it was no wonder that the health of the daughter of his people was not recovered. But there was a balm, and there was a physician, and therefore it was a wonder that there was no medicine administered, and no recovery.

Sometimes the Bible compares a nation to the body of a man. Here the nation of Israel is spoken of in an allegorical form as a daughter. When this way of speaking is employed, a number of things are attributed to a nation that properly belong only to a person, for example, head, heart, feet, and so on. You have this in the words of Isaiah, "The whole head is sick, and the whole heart faint. From the sole of the foot even unto the head there is no soundness in it" (Isa. 1:5-6). A few verses later the explanation is given, "Your country is desolate, your cities are burned with fire.... Thy princes are rebellious, and companions of thieves: every one loveth gifts, and followeth after rewards" (Isa. 1:7, 23).

By the head here, we are to understand the nation, or the rulers of the nation; by the heart, religious rulers; and by the words "from the sole of the foot even unto the head," all the people in general from the highest in the land to the lowest. The nation in its desolation is compared to the body of a man, sick, feeble, afflicted.

What was said of the nation of Israel can equally be said of our nation. She has been greatly honored by God with privileges, and yet so much have they been despised that we can ask concerning Britain what was asked about the Israelites, with the same reply. Is there no gospel in the land? Yes. Are there no prophets? Yes. Why do not the people believe? Or, is there no gospel and worship of God in the land? Are there no means to destroy sin in its moral influence? Yes. Are there no prophets and teachers sent by God to apply the medicine to them? Yes. Then is the country not coming to order as a result, nor any particular sign that the people are leaving their sins and returning to God? No. Well, why are they like this? Why are their sins not overcome, and their corruptions conquered? Why do they not submit in repentance, and bow in the dust before God so that they may be healed? This is the plain meaning of the words.

In the Scriptures, the condemnation and misery of men through sin is often described as pain, a plague, a wound, weakness, faintness, and so on. Indeed, there is a great likeness between them. Sin is similar to sickness in a number of ways.

1. The common cause of every sickness is some disorder in the body. Sickness is physical disorder. Some part of the earthly tabernacle decays. Some of the wheels of the intricate machinery do not function properly; they are driven too violently because of unnatural excitement; the heart beats too quickly in its astonishing task of pumping blood through all the vessels of the body, or perhaps too slowly. Perhaps the natural bodily fluids are dried up. There are many reasons unknown to us which account for the failure of the body. So it is spiritually with sin. Sin is disorder in the soul. Illness is something internally wrong with the body, and the confusion of sin is also internal. The understanding has been darkened, the will has become stubborn, the memory has been shattered and cannot retain good things, the affections have become carnal and earthly, the conscience has become sleepy and partial. In a word, all the instincts and faculties of the soul have been disturbed and warped through sin, and this accounts for all the disorder that is seen about us.

2. Sickness destroys the beauty of men and causes their glory to wither. Many lovely faces and handsome features have been marred by sickness and have been transformed into a likeness fit only for the grave. In exactly the same way the disease of sin has spoiled souls and brought to ruin the beauty of mankind. Man is not now like that which he once was. He is not now any more like Adam before the fall than a man afflicted by illness is to a healthy man. And not even the second Adam appeared in such beauty as the first Adam when he came from the Creator's hand, because our weakness was upon Him, and the chastisement of our peace and our sins weighed heavily upon Him. As for us, we are not like Adam in his perfection, and the most godly man on the earth is not to be compared to him. So little are we like him, so much have we been disfigured and blemished through sin, that we are scarcely rec-

ognized. Man was once in the image of God, but what is he like now? "There is none that understandeth, there is none that seeketh after God. They are all gone out of the way, they are together become unprofitable; there is none that doeth good, no, not one" (Rom. 3:11-12). They have lost their primal loveliness, and the image which they all now bear by nature is that of those who are ready for the second death.

3. Sickness restricts the usefulness of men; it unfits the man under its influence for any task or calling and utterly prevents him from being of any use in the world. Sickness sometimes develops to such a degree as to throw a person's senses into confusion, and drives him to speak nothing but foolishness. The man in his bed, poor creature, boasts about what he does, and all he does is unruly and disordered. So it is spiritually with the sickness of sin. It disables man from doing anything for the glory of God and impedes him from being of any use to his fellow creatures. It also robs men of their sense and understanding of spiritual matters, so that they are so foolish as to speak much of their works and all their accomplishments. The more they talk of what they can do, the less able are they to do anything. The sickness of sin destroys the usefulness of men, and makes them completely unfit for any spiritual task or duty.

4. Sickness makes men discontent and restless. When they are sick, men are anxious and always ill at ease; they want to be moved from room to room or from bed to bed, confusedly thinking that if they were in another bed or in another place they would feel better. The truth is that there would be no use in their being moved unless the sickness were moved. This is how it is spiritually with men suffering from the sickness of sin: they move here and there, sometimes from one religious persuasion to another; from immorality to self-righteousness; from sinful display to empty boasting and Pharisaic morality, all the while thinking that they will attain contentment. The truth is that the evil and the source of the restlessness is in ourselves, and for this reason there is no ease until the infirmity is

removed, nor peace to the conscience until the blood is applied. This is the balm that heals.

I intend to make three observations arising from the text, and I urge you to pray that the Lord will bless them to bring some to feel their affliction, and to see their need of the Physician.

    I. Various sicknesses that are normally found among men
    II. There is a physician and medicine
    III. The people are not yet cured

I. First, these are some of the spiritual illnesses most commonly found among men at present.

One dreadful sickness is *ungodliness*. Perhaps I do not need to preach that here, since I assume that there are not many such listening to me, if indeed any at all. Mercifully, there are not many in our country generally, but they are more frequently to be found in France, Spain, and distant lands. However, apart from a public, confessed atheism there is a secret atheism. There are even in this religious land more atheists in heart and attitude than can be imagined. The fool says in his heart, "There is no God," as if to say either that there is no God of any kind, or if there is, to wish that there were no God.

"Are you suggesting that there is anyone in this land of the gospel as ungodly as that?" Do not be angry with me for telling the truth. Although men do not say this with their tongues, yet there are many who live their lives as though there were no God, and that is practical atheism. There are two kinds of atheism: theoretical and practical. If there are not many of the first kind, who openly profess their opinion that there is no God, there are thousands who behave as if it were so. They are careless about their conduct, cherishing wicked thoughts in their minds, and committing sins secretly as if there were no omniscient God to search the heart and the mind, who sees in the dark as He does in the light.

A life without prayer and adoration of God is also atheism in practice. All who believe in God worship Him and pray to Him. Someone may object that I am judging too hard. I answer that it is impossible to judge too hard where sin is concerned. Can there exist a man calling himself a Christian, but neither praying to God nor worshipping Him? Are there prayerless saints? No such creature exists; it is a contradiction in terms. That man, instead of being a Christian is worse than a pagan. If pagans believe something to be God, they worship it. Not to worship, even according to pagans, is to act as if we had no God. In consequence, if there is a God, and we confess it, there is no reason not to pray to Him, nor to partake of a meal without asking His blessing or giving thanks, nor to have a home of our own without worshipping God. A prayerless life is an atheistic life.

One divine said that the curse of God was on the house without prayer, and that the man who lived in such a house was a pagan. You who are ungodly in secret, whatever your profession is, your attitude in private proves that you are an atheist, and shows beyond any argument that you do not believe in God who is present everywhere. You do things in secret that you would never do before this gathering, and yet you do them fearlessly before God who sees in the darkness. What is that, but unbelief in the omnipresent God? If you believed that there was a God, and that He is what He is, you would fear Him. If you believed that He was what He undoubtedly is, present everywhere and seeing in secret as in the light, you would be afraid of Him, even more than of ten thousand men. "If we are such great sinners as this, what will become of us?" Listen. There is a balm in Gilead. Is there a balm for such a dreadful sickness as this? Yes, there is. If your character is as black as that of the atheist, there is a balm offered in the Word of God with a healing power sufficient even for this.

Another dangerous illness is *ignorance of God, and a great darkness concerning the deep things of God.* It is difficult to preach to ignorant people because what is preached to them is not received, and there is no entry to the mind through the understanding. The result is that the truth does not remain there. "I remember a great deal," says someone. Maybe, but it is one thing to remember the words and to learn them and to recite them like parrots; it is quite another to understand them and to know those matters. There are many who can recite and remember things without knowing them. It is possible for men to learn the principles of religion like a parrot, but without being enlightened by them. I have heard about that remarkable bird that it can learn to say good and bad, but at the same time it has no idea of the one or the other, nor any concept of what it says. So it is with many who learn the things of God, learn them theoretically, learn the catechism or the words, but without understanding or grasping the matter.

Everyone who believes in God believes that He is great. And everyone who has seen the greatness of God is certain to be humbled to the dust. Those who see the beauty of Christ choose Him and accept Him. Those who believe that sin is evil leave it where it is. "But," says someone, "what if I am like that, without understanding and ignorant? What can I do? To whom can I go?" To that person I say, "Come to the physician in Gilead, and the incomparable balm that is there, and I am bold enough to say that one bottle of this will remove all the sickness and completely cure you."

The third sickness I refer to is *hardness of heart.* This is a fearful illness. What can be more dangerous to life than disease of the heart, on which all life depends? Hardness of heart is the worst of all the infirmities of the heart. Other sicknesses cause the heart to swell, or to race. This makes the blood vessels like bones. It is a truly terrible disease and extremely difficult to treat. But here is a Physician, and a balm that can cure the sickness and soften the stony heart.

Many are like this in a spiritual sense. They have heard the Word for years, but it has left no more impression on them than on the building where they meet. Their hardness is such that although the messengers of peace have preached the love of Christ to them, and the hatefulness of sin, and their great danger, and the richness to be found in the gift of God, they cannot be melted. Even with the hammer of God we cannot produce the slightest effect on their hearts. "Well," says someone, "there is no breaking of it, or treatment of it." But I assure you, there is. How? God with His own hammer can break in pieces the hardest heart in the world. Here is a physician who never failed to cure anyone, and if He takes them in hand they will be healed entirely. Unless this happens, it is a sickness that leads to the second death.

A fourth sickness which devours many is *worldly mindedness.* The mind and heart are set on earth, where our feet should be. I know of no natural illness that makes men walk on their heads. Yet this is the spiritual condition of all who suffer from this disease. Their heads and hearts are daily on the earth, whereas it should be under their feet. A natural and worldly disposition, the affections set on things that are below—these things have seduced and captivated you, turned you upside down, bound you to the earth, and are keeping you in the dark dungeon of the world. They will take you to utter darkness unless you are prevented by infinite grace. But the balm of Gilead deals with this! Therefore I cannot refrain from crying to you: dear people of the earth, drink freely of this balm, so that you may be cured and delivered from your indescribable peril.

There is yet another common affliction in the world, which is *formal worship:* "Having a form of godliness, but denying the power thereof" (2 Tim. 3:5). This consists of the body worshipping without the soul, religion of the knee and lip but not the heart. God has no appetite for such worship as this. The most eloquent preacher, the most gifted prayer, the sweetest singer are nothing but scoffers and blasphemers in God's eyes if they are devoid of the Spirit. If you sang as beautifully as Handel, and spoke as eloquently as the Apostle Paul, it would be nothing other than a mockery of God, without the Spirit. Today, thousands in Britain are like dead idols in the places of worship as far as spiritual life is concerned. All worship is formal without the Spirit, and there are more people involved in such worship than anyone imagines. Not many believe this now, but they will see it in the judgment when God comes to reveal the secrets of men and to search the hearts. May God awaken us to seek the cure; nothing but the balm of salvation can restore us.

There are also many other sicknesses that trouble only the saints. Here are some of them and I only mention them—wandering, uncontrolled thoughts, the plague of the heart, sinking under afflictions, lack of love to God and a failure to trust in Him, no appetite for the things of God, not even the sweet delights of the gospel and the feasts of salvation. These follow the saints while they are on the earth and trouble them greatly.

There are symptoms of death attending many infirmities. I will mention a few so that those who search themselves may recognize them. One of these signs is a combination of various sicknesses in the same person. This is a situation that has tested all the ability of many a skilled physician. That which would be sound treatment for one illness might be nourishment for another. The result is that the doctor who knows how to treat one illness independently of the other is frustrated when he comes to deal with both together. This is a case almost beyond human ingenuity. This is how it is with God's servants facing similar circumstances, often at a loss to know what to do and how to apply the balm for the recovery of the sick. They are unsure how to dispense it to the people because their diseases are so many and so varied. If they preach that which eliminates a legal spirit, an antinomian spirit is encouraged. If they give a dose to treat this heady antinomian spirit, a legal spirit rises in its place. This is a hopeless task for minor physicians. There is no one sufficiently skilful apart from the good Physician Himself. Let us therefore call upon the Lord Jesus, the best Physician, to administer medicine to such people.

Another unhappy and fatal symptom is that the patient has a great thirst, especially if the thirst persists over a long period. The balm and Physician of Gilead are more than sufficient for these also. It is no wonder if the preachers fail, because we are nothing but apprentices under the Chief Physician, who cares for all the sick throughout the vast infirmary. In a moment He can quench the strongest thirst, and quell the strongest desire. He can moderate men's thirst for legitimate things and overcome completely their thirst for unlawful things. He can prevent the evil by removing its cause.

A particularly bad symptom is that the patient cannot endure the light. This is a sign that he is very weak and that infirmity has almost ended his life. They shift very well in the night, but when morning breaks, they must close the curtains to keep out the light. It is a very bad sign in a spiritual sense when listeners cannot endure the light of the Word, and complain that the sermons are too searching. When the ministry exposes the deceitfulness of the hypocrite, and the divine light penetrates to his secret room, and identifies his deceit and his hidden wickedness, unless he is convicted, it will be unbearable for him, and he will cry out, "Keep out the light. Close the curtains over the windows of the ministry. The light is too strong for me; I cannot stand it." Wherever this is seen it is a sad symptom. Humanly, there is little hope of the recovery of the patient. But we do not give up while there is life, for what men cannot do, God can.

The next symptom I observe is extreme drowsiness, a sleeping sickness. The person is so overcome with sleep no medicine can keep him awake. In spite of giving him the most powerful medicine to rouse him, talking to him about his condition, warning him of his danger unless he awakes, the man continues asleep. All our efforts are in vain. Spiritually, there are religious people who are asleep. After the strongest sermon and the most pointed teaching from the mouths of God's servants, they remain asleep. Nothing has any effect upon him unless he has a visit from the good Physician. If the body is in danger from sleeping sickness, so is the soul from spiritual sleep. This condition of a religious man is frightening indeed—it is a fatal symptom. Let everyone who experiences it beware. Let us pray that God might bless some ministry to stir them while there is a means for them to be cured.

There is one further symptom which gives cause to fear for the sick person, and that is madness. This arises from the intensity of the illness: the fever increases until the blood boils, and the temperature rises and reason gives way to utter confusion. The affliction becomes too much for the man to bear. Similarly, there is such a thing as spiritual madness. A man is spiritually mad when he fights against God, and when he is so foolish as to think he can do anything to justify himself before God.

It is complete insanity to fight against God. Only a madman would go to fight against someone stronger than he is. Who but a madman would dance on the edge of the lake of fire, or would laugh heartily with the two-edged sword hanging over his head, dangling by a silk thread? The condition of spiritual madness is like this and much worse. Those who suffer from it are within the reach of the greatest danger, and reject the greatest good. They are entranced by pleasures when there is only a step between them and destruction. They laugh and joke while God sharpens His sword, and His indignation hovers above them with only the frail thread of their lives preventing it from falling upon them and killing them. What a dreadful state! Do they not care for anything? Yes, for the things of earth, but they are mad spiritually. They are very busy about the course and business of this world, and scarcely give sleep to their eyes as they strive for the dust of the earth and its worthless filthy rags, but they let go of the white garments and neglect the gold purified in the fire, which would bring them everlasting riches.

Similarly, it is insanity for men to speak of their abilities, and the miracles they have performed, and to make a great noise concerning their power and virtuous acts, while they, poor souls, cannot do anything, and cannot move from their beds, let alone work. They are completely confused by this burning sickness. They are like a sick person who has lost his reason, saying that he is going to get up and go to work, but when he tries he cannot stand on his feet for a minute. How many there are in our country who turn from the righteousness of Christ because they think they can present their own righteousness, and who refuse medicine because they do not know they are sick. Almighty God, visit those poor people in their darkness and madness who refuse the best Physician. They are suffering from a deadly disease and yet scorn the only medicine. Cause that medicine to bring many to their senses, to feel their sickness, to see the need of being restored, and to cry for the balm that cures every disease.

II. There are two questions in the text: Is there a physician? Is there a cure? The answer to both is, "Yes." That is understood in the question. On a deeper level, there are two queries that are implied in the words: Who is the physician? What is the cure?

In answer to the first, the physician is in one sense the Holy Trinity, since each of the persons has a part in the healing work. The Father designed the cure, the Son prepared it, and the Spirit applied it. In another sense, however, and perhaps the more relevant, the physician is God the Son. Jesus Himself said, "He hath sent Me to heal the broken-hearted." In the Epistle to the Hebrews, we read that "he is able also to save them to the uttermost that come unto God by him" (Heb. 7:25). In another place, He is spoken of as the one who is mighty to save. In the days of His flesh, He healed every sickness and illness that afflicted the people. He is infinitely suited to be a physician for all kinds of diseases, and that for a number of reasons. Here are some of them.

He has been anointed to that office. He has been set apart by the ordination of the highest court. He has been ordained and separated to the office of physician by God the Father to bind up those who are broken of heart. And in case anyone should think that He is a physician only to the rich, He has set up a sign to welcome the poor to Him, those who have no money, or any value. Because He has been ordained to preach to them, the poorest, weakest, most unworthy can come to Him without any fear that they will be turned away. The poorest among the sick can come to Him without any presumption, and that as often as they wish, and there is no danger of His reproaching them for their poverty, or of His telling them that they come too often. None of the servants have any right to turn you away because you are poor, and no angel in heaven can insult you when you come to His door, and say, "What are you doing here?" It does not matter what is your sickness, your weakness, your lowliness, your poverty; if you are ill, that is fitness enough. He is a good, gentle, sufficient, unfailing Physician, and infinitely suited to us.

Another reason why He is fitted for the work is that He has a good understanding of illnesses and identifies them perfectly. He is well acquainted with the sickness of everyone who comes to Him.

What other doctor could ever make this claim apart from Christ, the best Physician? Many skilful doctors have had to give up on their patients for lack of understanding the disease. Indeed, to be perfectly plain, many have killed their patients while trying to cure them because of a lack of knowledge about the case and a lack of understanding of the illness. But Jesus is fully acquainted with every sickness; He is aware of the spiritual affliction of every man, and He completely understands the diseased condition of our hearts. And blessed be God, He is able to cure us.

Again, He is qualified to be a Physician because He is gentle and merciful. Along with everything else that commends Him, He is exceptionally tender. He is merciful in attending to the plight of the poor sick people, and in listening to their complaints, and kind in treating their sicknesses. He is astonishingly merciful and compassionate, and prepared to undertake the cure of the worst cases imaginable, even of those who have nothing to pay. He presses Himself on the poor and is merciful to them in their trouble. He saw the impotent man at the edge of the pool with no one to put him in the water, and asked him, "Wilt thou be made whole?" and healed him of his infirmity. I wish I was alive then, says some sick person. What is that you say? You have as good an opportunity today as ever. He is here today, calling on you, and asking you through His servants the same question. Their words to every sick man or woman in the congregation are, "Wilt thou be made whole?" Jesus is saying, as it were, "I am ready to heal you, and My heart is full of pity. There is a sincere welcome to poor, weak people to come to Me for healing. Come to Me, everyone, so that your souls might live."

A fourth virtue He has as a doctor is His great patience. He has infinite patience in sympathizing with peevish, grumbling patients. They are often impatient, quarrelsome, complaining, and ungrateful, speaking to Him in a surly and arrogant way although He is so tender, because they are subjected to the treatment essential for their recovery. But He bears with them and endures them remarkably. What a wonderful Physician!

Then there is His ability to heal and His authority over the sicknesses. In this He excels everyone. He can control and command sicknesses as He wills, as a master rules his servants. He can say to one illness, "Come," and it comes, and to another, "Go," and it goes. Here is great comfort for sick people.

The second query is: What is the cure? Is there a balm? Yes. What is it? That balm is the blood of the Physician. Let heaven and earth be astounded! There are many doctors who are generous enough with the blood of the patients, but here is an incomparable mercy, and love to the sick without equal, that the Physician gives His own blood! He gave His blood as balm to cure the sick. "The blood of Jesus Christ his Son cleanseth us from all sin" (1 John 1:7). This is the blood that cleanses, and the balm that makes the most desperately ill well again. Here is a Physician who can raise the dead to life, and restore the most mad and disordered to a sound mind.

He has many devices and instruments for applying the balm. One of them is the Bible, His dispensary. All the words, testimonies, commands, threatenings, and promises are like many full bottles of medicine, showing the endless virtues of His blood. My fellow-sufferers, drink deeply of this so that you may be healed! There is a way in which you can be made better, whatever your complaint. Poor sick one, come boldly; here you can be restored and made completely well.

Another means is preaching. Preachers are like apprentices dispensing the drugs according to the needs of the patients, and applying them to the spiritual sicknesses of their hearers. We are often afraid that we have rushed carelessly into this important work without being called, and although we have been called that we have failed to divide the Word of truth. We are often afraid that a sermon is unsuitable for the hearers. Perhaps there are too many threats in it so that it discourages the weak, or too many comforts so that the arrogant are made complacent.

You, the most gentle in the church, do not know the half of the storms that beat upon us, and you cannot imagine the trembling experienced by the least of God's true servants. But the good Physician is able to correct all our mistakes. He cares for us, and super-vises all our work with His keen eye and suits the medicine to every case with His own hand.

There is another method which He frequently employs, and that is prayer. Those who pray have a great part in this. They are a kind of missionary or messenger in the service of the good Physi-cian. Some of them, especially those faithful in prayer, are very swift, and very useful, like speedy animals, in carrying messages from the sick to the Physician. If God sometimes leaves His people, or appears to leave them by withdrawing His presence and beams of comfort, those who pray feel it immediately. They give Him no peace. They knock at His door every day, and like the elect in the book of Revelation, call on Him day and night. Hardly a day goes by without their coming to Him on behalf of someone or other, representing the condition of some sick person who is about to die.

It may be that in some large hospital there is a room where only students or junior doctors have been for a number of days. The patients begin to complain and to say, "The chief physician has not been here for a long while." The condition of some of them grows worse until it becomes necessary to send an urgent message for the doctor himself. So has the prayer of faith often been instrumental in the healing of the sick. Is there anyone here longing for the Physician, and regarding the time long before He appears? Have you sent a request of late that He Himself should come? The most accomplished servants of themselves can cure nobody, nor the stu-dents or those receiving instruction. If you are seeking only us, finding us will do you no good whatsoever, because the disease will surrender to nobody but the Lord Jesus. And if you are satisfied without Him, no wonder that you are ill. How can you get better unless you turn to Him? We are not the doctor, just some little ser-vants under Him, who proclaim His power and invite men and women to Him and distribute the medicine that is in His Word. Sinner, go past us to our Master, the one we proclaim, that you may make a recovery and be healed.

III. There are various reasons why the sick are not healed. Christ is a Physician without His equal, and has been set apart and ordained for the work of a Physician. His blood is like balm, full of virtue, and able to save to the uttermost, and sufficient for every disease. His messengers are out declaring His ability so that none of the sick are ignorant of Him. Why, then, is not the daughter of my people cured of her sickness? Why does not everyone believe in Christ? Why does not everyone run after Him? How can it be that whole congregations, every soul at the invitation, do not come to the Son of God to be healed? How is it that we speak so often without witnessing healing, and why? Not because there is no Savior; you hear Him proclaimed each Sabbath. This is not because there is no virtue in His blood, nor because He is not able and willing to save to the uttermost.

How can I express my feelings? The all-knowing God knows how my soul is burdened for the multitude. You have been listening to the gospel for years; the balm and the Physician, the Savior and salvation are still within your grasp, and yet many continue without recovery. And if this is how you end your stay on earth, you will be forever held by the second death. Why does it have to be so? Why is not the health of the daughter of my people healed? The reasons are many; let me mention some of them.

In the first place, they are not cured because they do not feel their sickness and are not even aware that they are ill. Blessed Jesus, the good Physician! How is it that Thou art held in such low esteem by self-righteous, pharisaical men? It is because they are healthy in their own eyes, and they that are whole do not need a physician, but the sick. But if our dear Physician were to come to the worst congregation to dispense some of His divine merit and grace to the people, that would be enough to revive them, to move upon them in their lack of feeling, and bring them to feel their condition and see their need of salvation. Almighty Lord, we pray that Thou wouldst come in our midst and manifest Thyself clearly in the services. Through the ministry of the gospel move from one careless sinner to another with Thy work of grace until a great company are awakened to see their state.

Another reason why so many are not cured is that they love their sicknesses. There is enough healing medicine on hand, but in spite of all this, they do not get better because they take pleasure in their sins. Because of love for their sickness and their delight in sin, they refuse the balm and hate the Physician, despise Christ, the best Physician, who prepared salvation out of love for the sick ones and matchless mercy to poor sinners. There is a way they can be healed by being turned and given a nature that enables them to love Christ and His blood. Then the illness loses its power. And I am happy to see, if I am not mistaken, a good indication of that already on many here tonight.

A further reason why men do not get better is that they mix their own and the Physician's drugs, combining their own rubbish with the healing medicine of the Son of God. They add their poor, worthless efforts to His perfect obedience and righteousness, and so make all the work of no account. Christ does them no good. If you mix your efforts or your tears, your merits and your sufferings, or anything else with the blood of the Surety, everything He has done will be in vain for you. "If ye be circumcised, Christ shall profit you nothing" (Gal. 5:2). All His achievement, as far as you are concerned, will be of no avail.

Again, one of the reasons why the disease persists is the unwillingness of the patients to submit to the treatment. They refuse to obey the directions of the Physician. Taking up the cross, mortifying sin, laying corruptions on the cross—these tasks are all too demanding. Many find them drugs too bitter to take. But this is the only way to life, and there is no way to recover but by obeying the Physician. Let us cry for grace to obey and to submit to the treatment, so that we may be cured.

The final reason I give why people are not healed is that they mistake the time, like the man who has been ill for a long period, and has tried to cure himself, and refused to give in and see the doctor. When he is about to die, it is too late. The time the doctor usually spends in treating those who suffer from the disease has already passed. The man is lost because there is no more time. "O!"

says the sick man, "can't I be cured? Is there no hope for me?" The doctor replies, "I could have saved you if you had called for me sooner, and if I could have taken the matter in hand earlier, but now it is too late." But thank God, you are in time tonight, and it is an acceptable time for everyone here. Beware that you do not delay any longer, in case it becomes too late for you.

There is one last observation I wish to make. There are some who, in spite of everything, are getting better, even in these hard days. Some are still having the blood applied. The prospects are bright for many who are diseased. The thirst no longer rages; they begin to come to their senses, and to feel their illnesses. My advice is this. You who have received the benefit of the balm, seek it again. Swallow many doses of the medicine—there is no danger of your taking it too often. Those who have taken it are looking well—the insanity has almost entirely gone, so that they now feel what they did not feel previously. Many are better in every respect, and there is every indication that they will be perfectly well by and by, when they bid an eternal farewell to every sickness, without one disease or sickness to trouble them further.

What infinite love is displayed in the divine scheme! The Physician dies for His patients, and gives His blood as a balm to cure their infirmities. Although the love shown is so great, there are still some who are so hard as to despise it. They are in such darkness that they will not seek the healing that comes from it, and so refuse their own salvation.

Dear Jesus, come tonight among the sick ones, that a transformation may take place. Infinite God, have mercy on the multitude, hasten to deliver them, save the lost before it is too late, and through applying the balm, save many whose illnesses are fatal. Amen.

God Attending to the Contrite in Spirit

"But to this man will I look, even to him that is poor and of a contrite spirit, and trembleth at my word."
—Isaiah 66:2

When a man whom we account great and wise bestows praise on anything, a desire arises in us to possess that thing for ourselves. If a dear friend of ours exhorts us to seek for something, we do all in our power to acquire it for his sake. In this text, there is a description of true religion. It has the approval and praise of God, who is infinitely wise. Everyone who is His friend longs to please Him by seeking it. The essence of that religion is a poor and contrite spirit.

Let us look first of all at the way the words are introduced. "Thus saith the Lord, The heaven is my throne, and the earth is my footstool: where is the house that ye build unto me? and where is the place of my rest? For all those things hath mine hand made, and all those things have been, saith the Lord" (Isa. 66:1-2). It is as if the Lord was saying, "You are thinking as men naturally think when you suppose that the temple you built is enough religion for you. What is the temple to Me? No temple can contain Me. The vast heaven is but a little stool for Me, and all the earth just a place on which to rest My feet. If I needed a temple, I could make My own in a minute by the word of My mouth. Or I could enlarge the face of the earth as a floor for My temple, and extend the heavens far wider than they are as a roof for it. I could set the sun, moon, and stars—the great lights of heaven—as lamps to illuminate it. But the truth is that the whole creation cannot contain Me. In a word, I could not make a temple that would contain Me. I set no value at all on temples that are the work of men's hands."

Well, then, of what, Lord, dost thou take account? "To this

man will I look, even to him that is poor and of a contrite spirit. True religion and those who practice it are a thousand times more valuable to Me than your precious temple." One poor and contrite in spirit is of far greater worth in the sight of God than all the famous temples found on earth.

"To this man will I look." Does the Lord say, "To these men"? No. Followers of this religion are so few and far between that it is impossible to refer to them as "these." There are many in name, but few in truth. I have to pass by many who have a name for praying, praising, yes, and preaching too, before finding one like "this man." This man is poor, contemptible, sad, and weak. He is like the man in the parable to whom the Pharisee referred scornfully as "this publican." Others consider him not worthy of their attention; yet it is to this one that Jesus looks, and only to this one. He says, as it were, "All the mere followers and adherents of religion in the world mean nothing to Me, but 'this man' is precious to Me. I do not look on him along with others. I take no pleasure at all in any beside him. I will give them over to devils, and all the religious people in the world to hell fire, unless they are changed."

Here is the only religion acceptable to God and which has any worth in His sight. The observations from these words I have in mind are as follows:

I. Who are the poor and contrite in spirit?
II. A contrite spirit and a broken heart are precious to God
III. Why, based on reason and Scripture, they are precious to Him
IV. Counsel as to obtaining a contrite spirit

I. Who are the poor and contrite in spirit?

What are we to understand by this description? Who is the "poor" man? He is one who has been broken, crushed, bruised, and wounded; one who has been pricked in his heart at the sight of his sins and an awareness of them, and at the sight of Christ suffering for them; one who has been trampled under the hooves of the law and felt the benefit of the gospel; one who feels, in a manner of speaking, that there is no health nor soundness in him.

II. The great value of a contrite and broken spirit in the sight of God

God praises this kind of religion, and it is important to possess a religion that is honored by God. "Circumcision is that of the heart, in the spirit, and not in the letter; whose praise is not of men, but of God" (Rom. 2:29). Again, in 2 Corinthians 10:18, Paul says, "For not he that commendeth himself is approved, but whom the Lord commendeth." These are the ones that God praises in His Word more than any other, the poor and contrite in spirit. I intend to prove to you from reason and Scripture that the contrite spirit and the broken heart are pleasing and of great worth to God.

These are the sacrifices of God. "For thou desirest not sacrifice" (that is, of animals) "else would I give it: thou delightest not in burnt offering." But, "the sacrifices of God are a broken spirit: a broken and a contrite heart, O God, thou wilt not despise" (Ps. 51:16-17). Notice the form of the words: it is not the sacrifice, but the sacrifices of God that are spoken about. This is a reference to all the performances of the professors of religion to show that neither preaching, praying, hearing, singing, nor any of your works or religious deeds are acceptable sacrifices to God without a broken heart and a contrite spirit. Indeed, your worship and endless round of religious duties are abhorrent to Him apart from this. Without this spirit your singing, hearing, and praying are but a stench in the nostrils of the Lord of hosts. Apart from this, all our preaching will be rejected, and your hearing unacceptable. Everything we do is unacceptable and fails to meet with God's approval unless accompanied by a broken spirit. This is essential to all our offerings.

Here I draw attention to three matters:

1. The Lord prefers this to all the expensive sacrifices men with whole hearts can bring to Him. These sacrifices are of more worth to God than all the valuable offerings of old. We see this from Psalm 51 and elsewhere—"Thou desirest not sacrifice...thou delightest not in burnt offering." What does He desire? "The sacri-

fices of God are a broken spirit." The sacrifices of a broken heart are approved by God more than all the most costly sacrifices that ever were offered.

2. The breaking of the heart and the submission of the poor mean far more to God than the apparent, superficial submission of all the carnal professors of religion in the world. Mere outward display, such as wearing sackcloth, bowing the head, or rending the garment and the like are utterly worthless in God's account without inward repentance. Make yourselves presentable within through humility, and "rend your heart, and not your garments" (Joel 2:13). It is as if God was saying, "I would rather see one broken heart before Me than all the rent garments, and sackcloth and ashes."

3. The Lord prefers this sacrifice or attitude to all the detailed service of a formal pharisaical religion. Think of the parable of the Pharisee and the publican. Looking at these two, and judging by the outer appearance, almost everyone would say that the Pharisee was the more virtuous and the more gifted in prayer. Yet it was the poor, afflicted, contrite publican who went home justified, and not the other.

Another reason which shows that a broken heart is precious in God's sight is that this spirit is one of the invaluable features included in his promise. In Jeremiah 31:33, Ezekiel 11:19 and 36:26 we read that God will take away the stony heart and give His people a heart of flesh, that He will write His laws in their hearts and in their minds, and that they would be to Him a people and He would be a God to them.

Furthermore, the broken-hearted man is bound to be of great worth to God for God Himself has promised to be a physician to him. Psalm 147:3 reads, "He healeth the broken in heart, and bindeth up their wounds." Who is the one who does this? The Lord is the one. Your Physician is quite insignificant, is He not? By no means. He is the one who counts the stars, calling them all by their names. He is the one who covers the heavens with clouds and holds the sea in His palm. Our Physician is mighty—the Lord whose power is immense and whose understanding is past telling. Who heals the broken in heart and binds his wounds? None other than he. Is it some famous servant? No; no less a person than the Physician himself! Just as a skilled and famous doctor whose close friend is ill, and under his care will not entrust him to the care of an assistant or apprentice but will attend to him himself, so it is with the Physician of sinners. He will not send angels or saints to this task. He trusts no one with the work of saving the broken in heart because they are His loved ones. Perhaps some servant may be allowed to carry a bottle from Him to them, but no one other than He may administer the medicine.

Also, it is certain that such people are precious to God because He has promised to dwell with them. The psalmist says, "Though the Lord be high, yet hath he respect unto the lowly" (Ps. 138:6). Isaiah 57:15 says that although God dwells in the high and holy place, He dwells also with him that is of a contrite and humble spirit. High enough or low enough, God chooses to be there, either in the height and in glory or in the humble cottage of the poor in spirit. The Lord will not have somewhere in between; He must have exclusive possession of the rooms of the heart or nothing. God will not cohabit with the devil, and there is no communion between Him and Belial. He will not dwell with false professors, nor with the false presumptuous serpents who are nothing but religious hypocrites. God does not make a home for Himself with the arrogant and proud—He knows the proud afar off—but with the lowly and afflicted in spirit. He has desired these for His dwelling. "To this man will I look." This is the man I will observe; in him I will delight, of him I will take account, to him will I turn My face, and on him will I bestow approval.

Let us look at three thoughts concerning the words, "this man":

1. This is the man I will observe. My eye will follow him everywhere and I will watch over him whenever his spirit is troubled. When he groans in the depths, and sighs in the prisons; when his sins have overpowered him; when he is surrounded by his enemies

so that he cannot draw breath—then will I attend closely to him and will defend him.

2. This is the man in whom I will delight. I love no one more than I love him. No professor of religion pleases Me except this one. I love to hear the sound of his knocking and of his voice crying at My throne.

3. This is the man of whom I will take account. There are on the vine many leaves that are blown into the ditch, and many branches that bear no fruit that are thrown away to be burnt. But this man is the substance of the vine. Those like him are My true church, and them I will make My possession.

4. This is the man on whom I will bestow approval. I will be careful to acknowledge him. I will commend him, I will choose him, and I will make it plain to others that I love him. I will show Myself to him, I will cause My face to shine on him, I will comfort him when he is troubled, I will be his God and he will be My peculiar possession. To this man will I look, to defend him in every kind of weather that he will encounter on his journey. I will keep My eye on him in the river of death; I will be with him in and through the deep waters, and I will bring him safely home.

III. Why the poor and afflicted are so beloved of God
There are four reasons for this:

1. Because they give their hearts to God and it is for the heart that God asks
2. Because they are without guile; God holds dear those whose religion is without deceit
3. Because their affliction springs chiefly from a sight of Christ crucified
4. Because they are humble, and it is the humble professors of religion that God loves

1. God longs for the heart, and He loves these because He has their whole heart. In Proverbs 23:26, we hear the voice of God saying,

"My son, give me thine heart." This is the language of God for all who are here today. Oh, great and glorious multitude, will you give your hearts to God? God has come without question to our meeting according to His promise, although He is not so evidently in our midst as on previous occasions. Yet He is here, even if it is at the borders. We have not been left entirely without a sense of His presence throughout the meeting. But this is what I have to say: Do you know why He has come? What is His errand? He has come to seek for your heart and mine. Now, let me be so bold as to ask you: Has His errand been a success? I ask each one of you individually: has His errand been successful in your case? I imagine someone ready to say, "My heart is not worth giving; it is desperately wicked. You do not know it. It is harder than adamant and its misery is from hell." He does not ask what your heart is like—He simply says, "Give it to Me" as it is. Give it to Me without delay; give it to Me without waiting to make it better. The Lord says through the prophet, "Forasmuch as this people draw near me with their mouth, and with their lips do honour me, but have removed their heart far from me" (Isa. 29:13). I say with great earnestness, Oh, Lord! What dost Thou have against my dear listeners? Lord, they have been here from morning until evening. They arose at daybreak to hear the Word of life, and have continued until nightfall. Dear Lord, what dost Thou have against them? "Their hearts are far from Me." We can see no fault in them—their demeanor is sober, they listen intently, their generosity to your cause and their tenderness are beyond expectation. "But, in spite of it all, they have never given their hearts to Me." Again the Lord says through the prophet Ezekiel, "And they come unto thee as the people cometh, and they sit before thee as my people, and they hear thy words...but their heart goeth after their covetousness" (Ez. 33:31). My people, God requires the heart!

2. These are pleasing to God because they are without guile. None are more genuine and sincere than those who are poor in spirit, and a religion without pretence is of the utmost importance to God. He loves truth within, and takes pleasure in purity in His children. It is

truthfulness in the heart and uprightness in principle that He requires. These are those of whom it can be said, "Behold an Israelite indeed, in whom is no guile!" (John 1:47). This is why He loves them. If only I could express what is on my mind just now. These people, poor and afflicted in spirit, have been dealt with in such manner that there is no way for them to entertain deceit or for falsehood to remain in them. The lightning of Sinai has struck them—the arrows of the Word have wounded them—and every joint pierced by the sharp, two-edged sword. The weapons of God have crushed them and the hammer of divine truth in the hand of the Spirit of God has beaten every inch of them, so that it is impossible for them to contain deceit, hypocrisy, or anything of the kind.

3. God loves the contrite in spirit because their affliction springs chiefly from a sight of Christ crucified. Their grief is intense from looking at their sins, but as they look further, on Him whom they pierced, their grief is doubled. Great is their concern for the afflictions of Joseph. Their sorrow was very deep on the slopes of Sinai. But at Calvary it reached its peak as they beheld Christ crucified and bruised for their iniquities. And God loves those who love His Son; He comforts those who mourn for wounding Him.

4. He loves them because they are humble and self-effacing; this attitude is highly prized by God and is most seemly.

IV. Some directions as to how this spirit may be obtained

I imagine I can see a great company beside themselves with a longing and desire to possess this spirit, and ready to cry out with one voice, Oh, Lord, what shall we do in order to have this spirit? Is there any way in which I can make it mine? If there is anyone like this present, thank God I have authority to answer: Yes, there is a way, and it is for such as you. To the hard-hearted, the promise is for a tender heart; therefore, I counsel you to seek it; and in order that your search may be successful, let me give you three exhortations: First, seek it from God. He delights to see such as you at His throne, and it will please Him to hear you asking for a broken heart. Second, seek it through Christ. This is where He has promised to meet in peace with the sinner, and through Christ, every helpless cry is acceptable. Third, seek it by pleading His promise to take away the stony heart and to replace it with a tender heart of flesh. Seek it in this way, and you will certainly receive it; He has never refused anyone who has sought it according to the manner He has decreed.

Here are some applications of these things, and some general observations arising from them.

1. Set your sight on the blood of the cross. Look from where you are to Jesus suffering in your place. See the rough treatment He received from the court of Pilate to the hill of Calvary. Hear His groanings in the garden. Consider the bitterness of His suffering and the intensity of His crying in the agonies of the death of the cross.

2. Be mindful of your many faults and your sins in the face of conscience and light, and your lies ever since you were a child. Look back a little on your life, and perhaps you will remember one out of a thousand, and of your idle words one out of ten thousand, and of your wicked works, one out of a million. But know this, although you may have forgotten them, God does not forget. They are in the book of His remembrance. He beholds the good and the bad, in the darkness as in the light. Consider the number of your sins without repentance, and be amazed that you are not in hell.

3. Think hard about the wages of sin, and the wrath of God revealed from heaven against all ungodliness and unrighteousness of men.

4. Consider the judgment to come and the minute account you have to give if you go there without being changed.

5. Look to eternity and to the fact that you will be there in one of two conditions; and ask yourself in all seriousness, "What? Shall I go there without faith in Christ?"

6. Observe the ordinances and frequent the means of grace. Choose

and love the ministry that will shake your bad foundations, and the most fervent sermons, and the most sincere and pointed preachers.

7. Pray often, pray often in secret and say, "Lord, break my heart with Thy tenderness; wound my heart a little again in this service." Cry to Him again and again to give you that religion that is acceptable to Him. And do not give in until you prosper in your errand.

One or two words again to two kinds of people before I finish: to those whose hearts are whole and to those whose hearts are afflicted. First, to those whose hearts are whole: what hard people you are! Your hearts are sound and your spirits are whole and you have not been humbled by grace. God's weapons have never affected you at all. You who have been able to remain complete, in spite of all means employed by God and all His dealings with you. You who do not fear and are not pricked under the fiery ministry of Sinai, nor the threatening of the Almighty against sin. You whose hearts are not melted by the gracious proclamation of the gentle gospel and the infinite grace of Jehovah. Heed the warning in time. If you go on like this much longer, the effect of the wrath of God on you will be so dreadful that there will be no means of recovery. Then you will remember when it is too late, how many times Christ and His salvation were offered to you. But you took no account and did not profit in the least from His sacrifice. Rather, you refused the Physician who saves to the uttermost, and the Brother born for adversity. Oh pray, while God hears prayer, that He will break your heart by His grace, so that He will not have to break it by His indignation!

Next, to those whose hearts are broken, and to the afflicted in spirit. I love to speak of this. Oh blessed people, God loves to gaze upon you! But you say, "What, me? You have missed the mark entirely. Me, blessed? There is not a man in the congregation with a harder heart than mine, or one more miserable in his feelings. Indeed the hardness of my heart is my grief, and the health of my spirit is my concern every day!" Well, poor soul, do you not recognize your character yet? If this is how you feel, I am bold to say that you are the very person. You are the one in whom God delights, the very one who knows each plague of his own heart. And I have news to give you today. God has promised to restore you, and make you perfectly whole, and cleanse you from your plague forever.

Oh, that we would have more brokenness among us! How many there are whose hearts are still whole, in spite of all God's dealings! Where are the divine weapons, and the sharp arrows, and the dear hammer that breaks the rocks of flint? Where is the sharp, two-edged sword that separates the soul and the spirit, the joints and the marrow, and divides men from their sins? Oh God! Come with Thy weapons. Work graciously on souls. Show Thyself mighty through the ministry. Manifest Thyself in our midst. Break hearts with Thy love. Shatter with Thy grace many whole, hard, stubborn, wicked hearts. Work until the hardest are overcome. May it be so. Amen.

SERMON 10

God Choosing and Calling Men

"Ye have not chosen me, but I have chosen you, and ordained you, that you should go and bring forth fruit, and that your fruit should remain: that whatsoever ye shall ask of the Father in my name, he may give it you."
                                                                —John 15:16

The scheme of salvation in its entirety has been designed to remove pride and boasting from man; this is the reason why there is so much hostility on the part of man against the plan of salvation and God's way of saving man. Salvation is entirely and completely of God and exclusively of God's grace without anything contributed by man. It is not because of godliness or merit or the ability of man or any kind of goodness on his part. The sum and substance of the gospel is this: "Ye have not chosen me, but I have chosen you, that you should go and bring forth fruit." This truth is like two large veins running through the entire gospel, and if there is anything contrary to this, either in doctrine or experience or profession, there is something wrong. To oppose this is to strike at the very source of salvation. This is an essential truth: man is nothing and God is everything in his salvation. I can say of this text that this is the experience of every true Christian, and the sum of every correct doctrine. There can be no correct system unless it is founded on this principle.

These two veins run through the whole body of the plan of salvation. Every Christian feels this and says from the heart, "Not unto us, O Lord, not unto us, but unto thy name give glory." Salvation is so ordered that it brings man to the dust, and to bear fruit to the glory of God. God has no way of saving a man and leaving him fruitless. Everyone God saves He makes fruitful. It is impossible to have eternal life as the end unless holiness is the fruit now. God will bring no one to heaven at last unless he is fruitful here. All the working of grace tends to make man fruitful, and this too is the rule in the judgment: "Every tree that bringeth not forth good fruit is hewn down, and cast into the fire" (Matt. 7:19). Every unprofitable servant will be bound hand and foot and cast into outer darkness. God has no way of saving the unprofitable except by changing them. No branch that is unfruitful here, and continues to be so throughout life, will blossom in paradise. Utter darkness and everlasting fire awaits them on the other side if their days on earth were unprofitable and unfruitful.

How is it that there are men who have not chosen Christ and His salvation? Is not the scheme clear? Of course, it is perfectly clear, but men are by nature opposed to it, and therefore do not choose it. These words were spoken by Christ on the night of His betrayal. His listeners were all godly men without one hypocrite among them. My dear people, where will you find their equal? It was in this room that Christ had eaten the last supper with His disciples after Judas had gone out to betray Him to the chief priests. It was the disciples alone who were His hearers.

In this chapter, Christ exhorts His disciples to love, obedience, and fruitfulness. As He does this, He reminds them of different kinds of love: the love of the Father to Christ, the love of Christ to the disciples, the love of the disciples to Him, and their love to one another. Love is the most prominent feature in the whole plan of salvation, and that is the mainspring of our salvation. In a word, salvation is altogether love, from first to last. Love is the grace that makes the religion of the godly most distinctive. It is the love of God that shines most brightly in the plan of salvation, which is its prime motivation and is the foundation of it all. And it is love that shines most brightly in those who are saved after they have been transformed through grace. This is the root of their obedience to God and their love to Christ. The love of God for them is the foundation of their love for Him, as well as the foundation of their love for Christ and for one another. Love is the marrow of religion, and no religion is worth anything without it. No merit or virtue is a substitute for it. If we could speak with the tongues of men and of angels, if we had faith that could move mountains, if we fed the poor with our goods and gave our bodies to be burned, without love, it would be nothing. All would be unacceptable without love. Oh, precious grace—how sad that so many are without it who claim the name of Christian! As for all such who practice religion without the love of God, their work is vain, and will vanish completely, so that nothing will remain when they face the throne of God.

Next, Christ speaks of His own love for them. The fruit of that love was His appearance in the flesh. Because of His love for them, He gave Himself instead of them. Because of His love, He called them His friends, put His name on them, and chose them to be His own people. Then we have the text. The Lord Jesus did not mean by these words that the disciples did not love Him and choose Him. There is no question that they did choose and love Him. What He meant was, "It was not you who began to love, and it was not you who chose first. I was the first to love and to choose, and as a result of My love you were brought to love and to choose Me." There is no such thing as a godly man who does not love Christ, and every true Christian chooses Christ—he delights in Him and rejoices in Him above all else. But it is equally true that it was not they who were the first to choose. Although they choose and love, Christ began the work and persuaded them.

There are some observations I would like to make by way of exposition of the words.

"I have chosen you." Many theologians explain this choice by saying that Jesus was speaking of their selection as apostles. What they understand is that Jesus said, "You did not choose Me as teacher and master but I chose you as disciples and apostles, as missionaries and teachers to go out to preach and to publish My name among the Gentiles, and to be instruments in My hand and by My Spirit to spread My gospel throughout the world." That was an important choice, and no doubt will produce much fruit. It is certainly true, but it is not the whole truth. Although it is God who chooses men for the service of His house, it is not only for that work

that He chooses. That is obvious when we consider that Judas was not present when these words were uttered. In one place, Scripture says that Christ chose Judas, and in another place that he was not chosen, which shows clearly that there is more than one choosing. In John 6:70 it is said that Christ chose Judas as an apostle, "Have not I chosen you twelve, and one of you is a devil?" He said this of Judas Iscariot, the son of Simon, because he was about to betray Him, and he one of the twelve. Christ chose them all as apostles and ministers; they were ordained to high office and to a notable bishopric. But in spite of this, one of them was a devil, and so he had been all his life; he had never been anything better. This was his state when he was chosen as a disciple, and when he was ordained to go out to preach the kingdom of God. He was the son of perdition even on his best day. In John 13:17, 18 we read these words, "If ye know these things, happy are ye if ye do them. I speak not of you all: I know whom I have chosen: but that the scripture may be fulfilled, He that eateth with me hath lifted up his heel against me." When we remember that Judas was probably not in the room when the words were spoken, we cannot but see in them something more than being chosen for office. Those to whom the words were spoken were saved to eternal life and were made the children of God through adoption. Then again, as we consider the greatness of the love of God, some mighty act is necessary to demonstrate and prove the greatness of the love. For my part I do not think that choosing or appointing a man to an office is proof of such love. Calling a man to some office, however high that office, is not sufficient proof of the love of God for him, nor is the fact that a man has not been so called a proof of the displeasure of God. To occupy some position in the church, however exalted, is not in any sense a demonstration of the love of God to man. But if God wanted to show the extent of His love and His graciousness to sinners, He could not do it more clearly than by showing that He has chosen them to be His children, and to enjoy everlasting glory with Him. There are some remarks I wish to make in general on these words.

I. The choosing of men to office in the church, and the choosing and calling of them to true godliness and the power of religion, belongs to God alone, and not men

II. Those that God chooses and calls, He chooses and calls to bring forth the fruit of sanctification

III. The throne of grace is free to sinners conscious of their inability to produce such fruit, and at this throne they may find help to bear fruit to God, and to remain fruitful to the end

We shall consider this choosing in the two respects mentioned: the choosing to offices, and the choosing to the power of religion.

I. God chooses and calls

Let us first consider being chosen for office in the house and church of God. It was not on account of any exceptional qualities in them that they were chosen, but through the good will of God. There was nothing in Andrew, Peter, Matthew, or any of the disciples that distinguished them from their companions until Christ called them. There was nothing in them by nature, by learning, by grace, or in any other respect that raised them above the ordinary; if anything, they were worse than their peers. They were disciples of Christ: humble, inconspicuous, and despised. They were among the ordinary and common people of their neighborhoods, and some of them, before they were called by Christ, were ungodly and wicked, without one excuse to give to account for their works and to lessen their guilt. Nor did they have one reason of any kind to present for their being chosen to such prominence, apart from the good will of Him who had chosen them. It was not because of a lack of knowledge of them that they were chosen either, or failure to know the kind of men they were, for Christ was well aware of what they were, and knew them perfectly when He chose them. There was no virtue whatsoever in one of them that inclined Him to choose them. Not one of them was repentant, none of them was choosing Him; rather, they all felt they were happy and content without Him. Although they had nothing to qualify or commend them, and although Christ knew this perfectly well, and knew them perfectly well, He chose them to be His disciples, and after that to be apostles and witnesses to Himself, and instruments in His hand to carry His name throughout all the earth.

Whom does He choose? He chooses anyone He wants to choose. Whom He wills, He calls. There is a particular word to this effect in Mark 3:13, when He is choosing the twelve apostles: "And he goeth up into a mountain, and calleth unto him whom he would: and they came unto him. And he ordained twelve, that they should be with him, and that he might send them forth to preach." Here we see the principle on which He chooses. It was His will, His decree, His choice, that was His rule for placing men in positions, not whether they were genial or pleasant. It was not the best, most suitable, most virtuous in themselves, but those whom He willed that He called. The result of their being called was a ready obedience to His call. "They came unto him." Christ first chose, called, and took hold of them; and they then listened, obeyed, and came. In consequence of the call from Christ, they listened, obeyed, left their old paths, chose Him, and came to Him.

There is here a double choice; their choice is the fruit of His choice. There are some other pertinent words on this subject in Philippians 3:12: "That I may apprehend that for which also I am apprehended of Christ Jesus." There was not in any of those who were called any inclination or desire to be disciples of Christ, until He had chosen them; but because He had chosen them, they chose him. Similarly with the seventy: Christ chose them by His sovereign will to help the twelve apostles preach the kingdom of God. Again, it was not only He who chose officers in His house, but it is He who does so now.

It is Christ who shows now, as in previous ages, who are the ones He has chosen for offices and high places in the church of God. As many as Christ calls will come to Him. The responsibility for choosing men to positions in the church lies as much on Christ now as it did in the days of the apostles, and will remain so until the day the trumpet sounds. The church, the ministry, and the offices in the church will be the concern of Christ until the last judgment. This is seen very clearly in the important words we have in Ephesians 4:7-12, "But unto every one of us is given grace according to the measure of the gift of Christ. Wherefore he saith, When he ascended up on high, he led captivity captive, and gave gifts unto men.... And he gave some apostles; and some prophets; and some, evangelists; and some, pastors and teachers; for the perfecting of the saints, for the work of the ministry, for the edifying of the body of Christ." Here we see that every spiritual gift has been given for the service of the church and for its edification. But it is in Christ alone that they are treasured up. To Him belongs the appointment; to Him belong the choosing and adapting for the offices of the church from the time of His ascension to heaven until the time of His return on the clouds of heaven. It is in Christ and with Christ that the authority rests to appoint to every office and position in His house. No one has any gift that was not received from Christ and His fullness. Christ is the head and king of His church and will remain so until He comes on the clouds of heaven.

Are there not false shepherds, or prophets who have not been sent? It is possible for men to set in the church those who are officers in name only, who are carnal, without the Spirit. But I say that there is no man, body of men, bishop, deacon, teacher in an academy, or anyone else who can make one man profitable for the church of God but Christ. No one can be fitted for the work of the ministry, nor have any spiritual gift which God will own, for the perfecting of the saints and the edifying of the church, unless he has received it from the treasure and fullness of Christ.

The way Christ generally takes to show and raise those whom He chooses for office is by calling them, separating them early and equipping them for the work. Sometimes He chooses them from the womb, as in the case of Jeremiah: "Before I formed thee in the belly I knew thee; and before thou camest forth out of the womb I sanctified thee, and I ordained thee a prophet unto the nations" (Jer. 1:5). Frequently, indeed usually, when the Lord intends to use someone to do a great work for Him in the world, He separates him

early, adorning him with grace and spiritual gifts, and giving him
an abundance of natural ability for his work in the kingdom. The
Lord's attention is on him early; He knows him before he is born,
and sanctifies him in his mother's womb. Christ's attention is on
him before he exists, and before he does good or evil. He knows
him before anyone else knows him, or sees his virtues. He supplies
him with natural abilities as a man, and then adorns him with grace
and spiritual gifts. Later He calls him, drawing the attention of the
church to him, and infusing him with a love for the work. He creates a thirst in the members of the church to call him and set him
apart for the work, and when He has chosen him and placed him
in the work, He causes him to bring forth much fruit. The Lord
does not call anyone except to bear fruit: "Ye have not chosen me,
but I have chosen you, and ordained you, that ye should go and
bring forth fruit, and that your fruit should remain" (John 15:16).
If you see a man in an office in the church, whose life is wicked,
whose walk is inconsistent, whose service is unfruitful, you can be
sure that God has never called that man. Everyone whom the Lord
chooses is fruitful. This is a sure and infallible mark. When the
Lord called the twelve to be disciples, and made them apostles and
preachers, He put within them a godly zeal and fire and appropri-
ate qualities for the work as a proof of their apostleship and of their
choice and ordination by God. Much fruit was produced by them,
and it was lasting fruit. They were so full of the Spirit that heaven
was opened to some of them. They went out and preached everywhere, though their own abilities were poor, even so, the Lord
working with them, bestowing astonishing success on their ministry and achieving great things by them.

They were ordained to this calling to go and preach forgiveness of sins in His name and proclaim the kingdom of God among
all nations. God owned their work, and many who should be saved
were thereby added to the church. Through them, multitudes were
brought to God and called to be saints. What marvelous fruit! And
the fruit will remain in the church throughout the ages until Jesus
returns on the clouds of heaven. There will be yet more fruit on

their labor through the ages; through their work and labor, Jesus will see of the travail of His soul. A corn of wheat has fallen to the ground, and therefore, there is bound to be much fruit. What is the success throughout the nations which has attended the ministry? It is the fruit of the corn of wheat which fell to the ground and died, now making its appearance. The fruit of their work is the labor of the soul of Jesus being gathered. The guilty being acquitted; the prisoners being released; the unclean being washed and presented before the throne of God and the Lamb—there is much fruit on the earth now, and more to be gathered. Christianity still continues, and will yet increase in spite of all the efforts of Satan, his servants, and his instruments, to hinder and prevent it. On it will go, despite all the counsels of Satan against it. All the frogs of the bottomless pit can not destroy it. Although Tom Paine ridicules it and says it will fall of its own accord, it still continues, and the fruit of the labor of the twelve apostles is likely to fill all the earth.

Another former enemy of Christianity, David Hume from Scotland, said that before the passing of another five hundred years, there would be no trace of the foolishness of Christ and His cross. That man has long since gone to his own place and the period he indicated is passing away, but his prophecy is unfulfilled. We still have the task of preaching the gospel, and God, by the foolishness of preaching, still saves those who believe. We still have the fruit of the labor, and it will continue on the earth until Jesus comes the second time to judge the world. Not only was the work, labor, and message of the apostles fruitful—it will be fruitful. Is it not Jesus who chooses officers and ordains them to their ministry? How can they be unfruitful if it is He who has sent them? Will He not prosper them in the work they were sent to do? Will not His purpose be accomplished through them when He who sent them is able to do all things? For these reasons, it is absolutely certain that the good news will be effective in His hand to turn sinners to Himself, to turn them from darkness to light, and from the power of Satan to God.

Secondly, there is another choosing, which is more important than the first. This is the choosing to life, the call to be saints, and to true religion and godliness, and that early in life. There has been a choosing from eternity. To deny this would be to deny the omniscience of God together with a large portion of His Bible. The Bible abounds in references to this choosing. I am astonished that sensible men even deny the election of grace. There are hundreds of definite and unmistakable words in the Bible showing beyond dispute, apart from the choosing we have already considered, that there has been a choosing before time began, in eternity, before the existence of the world. And there is another choosing, which is the choosing in time, which is made according to that choice. All who are called are called according to His purpose. Is it not we who choose Him? No, not at first. If we were left to ourselves, we would never choose Christ, nor receive Jesus as Savior. We would choose the ways of sin, and we would continue along our sinful course, insisting on our ways, until they ended in destruction. One thing that proves this is the fact that men persist so long without repenting, and even do so despite the gentleness and patience of God. God spares, yet they harden their hearts. His servants call, and yet, they ignore.

It is plain to see that we would never come on our own account. We were hard enough (until God changed us) to face death without seeking the Savior. And we would have gone to the judgment, if we had been left alone, without knowing the Savior. We would have scoffed at the idea of salvation, and would have gone unprepared to the other world, without hope and without God in the world. It is not because of their goodness that anyone has been chosen. Those who have been chosen are not one bit better than others; God did not foresee anything commendable or virtuous in them. In the seventh chapter of Deuteronomy, we read, "The LORD did not set his love upon you, nor choose you, because ye were more in number than any people; for ye were the fewest of all people." God is said to have chosen Israel as a nation to put His name on them so that they might be a holy people to the Lord their God. The way in which this came about is this, "For thou art an holy people unto the LORD thy God: the LORD thy God hath chosen thee to be a special people unto himself, above all people that are upon the face of the earth" (Deut. 7:6). What excellence did they possess that marked them apart from other nations when they were chosen? Listen to His answer: "The LORD did not set his love upon you, nor choose you, because ye were more in number than any people; for ye were the fewest of all people" (Deut. 7:7).

So it is to this day. It is not because of any superiority in us, or because we are more attractive, or more holy, less sinful, or for any virtue in us or good works that we have performed that the Lord chose us. Well, what then? You were chosen because the Lord loved you. "Of his own will begat he us," when there was nothing good or attractive in us as a motive (James 1:18). Here is a workman choosing stone and wood for building. Perhaps he sometimes chooses material that is crooked and knotted. How can he produce something lovely from such materials? He has means for fashioning them to his purpose by sawing, carving, planing, cutting, and shaping them to size and measure so that they can be joined together and made attractive and fit for the place appointed them in the building. Our Architect has the means to do the same in a spiritual sense. Thank God for this. He can choose the twisted and misshapen, the filthiest sinner and the worst rebel possible, and perfectly beautify them, prepare them, and bring them together as lovely stones in the spiritual temple, without a mark or blemish on them, nor any trace of the ugliness they once bore.

"I have chosen you." It is He who chooses first. I have no doubt that there is opposition to this doctrine in the heart of the proud. This is because the idea of being chosen humbles the proud. There is a bitter war raging in the heart of the proud man, and a dispute against the scheme, because it humbles self. Rebellion rises in him because God chooses first. This is the case secretly even in many of whom better things might be expected. If we could search hearts, we would see in the religious world hundreds secretly fighting and quarrelling, wanting to deny the election of grace and the eternal purpose, the

most glorious and comforting doctrine in the book of God. The fact that God chooses is not according to their taste. The plan of free grace is unacceptable to man by nature, owing to the pride that is in his heart, and his hostility to anything that tends to overthrow pride. Even in the matter of his salvation he wants to have the praise and the credit for it himself rather than God. In a word, he wants to be God. This is the essence of the first poison, "Ye shall be as gods" (Gen. 3:5). But God insists on humbling all those who are saved, and all who are preserved to everlasting life He will bring to the same mind as that of the text. He will convict the man of his rebellion, his obstinacy, his enmity and opposition to Him and His scheme, his refusal of Christ and his despising of His name. He will persuade him to believe that he will go to eternal damnation if left to himself, and to confess that salvation is all of God.

Dear friends, I could enlarge on this until the sun sets! Why were Manasseh, Mary Magdalene, the thief on the cross, Saul the persecutor, and many like them saved, together with many of their brothers perhaps here today, whose names have been on the black list? Why do many who were despisers of the name of the Son of God and enemies of His now choose Him? Why and how did such a change come about? This is only because He first chose them. No other reason can be given! The text clearly states, "I have chosen you." I believe that there are scores present here who, if they could, would testify publicly to this truth. They would say with tears of love, "We would have lost our lives for ever, if left to ourselves, and there would have been no hope for us if it had not come from another quarter, that is, if He had not first sought us." Someone says, "I was the worst, the hardest, the dirtiest, the most unclean, the darkest that ever was born, the most careless concerning salvation, with no respect for righteousness or regard for the blood of the cross. I would never have chosen Christ. But it was through Him and of Him entirely that salvation flowed to me. It was the fire of the love of God that first warmed my cold heart-sparks of His love that He threw into my cold heart, first warming my icy soul, and giving me the first impulse of love to Him." "Ye have not chosen me, but I have chosen you."

II. The purpose of God in choosing was that they might bear fruit

Those whom the Lord chooses and calls, He chooses and calls to bear holy fruit. God inclines them and gives them a desire to go often to the throne of grace where there is strength available for them to produce fruit and to continue to be fruitful to the end. All those who are in Christ go after Him, they are separated from others and made a people becoming to Him and eager to do good works. Christ sets Himself apart and grants them the power of godliness. He has ordained them to bring forth fruit, and they are all created in Christ Jesus unto good works. The good works are like paths foreordained that they should walk in them. He plants them in His vineyard, and grafts them into the true vine, so that it is impossible for them not to bear fruit; and in Him they do bear fruit, by being in living union with Himself. It is from Him that they receive a gracious sap to bring forth fruit to holiness, to live to the glory of God and the benefit of their fellow-creatures. He delivers them from sin, and makes them servants of God so that the fruit may be holiness and the end may be everlasting life. They bring forth fruit to the glory of God the Father. They are aware of their own insufficiency and inability, and enjoy the grace of God as all else in their transformation, and are prepared to say as does the text, that it was not we who chose Him but He us, and gave us the means to produce fruit. It is He who gives them the means to flourish in His house and to be fruitful in His courts, just as the branch produces fruit by virtue of its unity with the tree, and receives sap from the tree causing it to bud and produce fruit of the same nature as the root. When they fall into sin or backsliding, He does not give them up but comes to them again if need be, visiting "their transgression with the rod, and their iniquity with stripes" (Ps. 89:32). He will convict them and restore them until they regard their sins as hateful, submit themselves, and glorify God. He will make their conviction and conversion as remarkable as their sin—apparent to the world and pleasing to the church of God. So they glorify God in the day of visitation.

What is his experience and attitude? He hates himself because of the poor quality of his fruit, the odium of his sins, the enmity and hardness of his heart against God. He rejoices at the thought of a Savior who destroys the works of the devil, and cleanses from every sin, who can cleanse even him so that he can live a holy life and be fruitful to the glory of God. Allow me to press upon you at present the necessity of self-examination: how is it with us in this matter? God forbid that any of us should deceive ourselves! The tree is known by its fruit, and so it is also with professors of religion. It is by their fruits that they will be known. It is impossible for us to have a holy religion unless we have holy fruit. It is a fearful and terrifying thing for us to be deceived in the most important matter of our salvation. We must have good fruit because it is the fruit that shows the nature of the root. Good fruit proves that the religion is good. "Every good tree bringeth forth good fruit; but a corrupt tree bringeth forth evil fruit" (Matt. 7:17).

III. That the throne of grace is free to all who feel their insufficiency and desire a means to be fruitful

The throne of grace is always free to the sinner conscious of his inability to produce fruit to God. Here there is help available to produce that fruit and to continue being fruitful to the end. Christ says, "Whatsoever ye shall ask the Father in my name, he will give it you" (John 16:23). In the previous verses, Christ had been speaking to the disciples about being fruitful, and in these words it is as if He wishes to restrain them in case they should think too highly of themselves. It is as if He was saying, "Although I have told you about the necessity of bearing holy fruit, you can produce absolutely nothing unless you receive it from My Father. It is from Him that you must have the power." He is telling them that no one comes to Him except him whom His Father in heaven draws to Him. This is to prevent them from thinking that they were great.

There is the same danger that we may become inflated. To prevent us from falling into this trap, let us turn to the mirror of the

Word and look into it. What is our character? What are we? Only weak, vain, and poor: nothing in and of ourselves. But in spite of our weakness, Christ declares Himself to be a Father, Brother, and Husband to His church, and in these capacities offers Himself to us. Take hold of My strength, He says, in the Son, and I will make a covenant with you. Seek godliness before you die. The only place to turn is to the Father, in the face of every frailty and poverty, unworthiness, corruption, and weakness of every kind. Here is the comfort: the throne of grace is now free and access possible through Him to God. Christ says, "Whatsoever you ask the Father in my name, believing, you shall receive." This is like saying, My name is always at your service, and it is enough to assure you of acceptance with God, and to secure for you deliverance from every tribulation, every cross, every enemy, every hurt and every wrong, and from care and trouble of every kind.

Whatever trial overwhelms you, whatever temptation wearies you, go to the throne of grace and there you will find a way to overcome all, and to triumph over them and sing in the water and the fire. Go to the Father in the name of Christ, to God on the throne of grace, and you will be enabled to go through the water without drowning and through the fire without being burned. You will be able to succeed in every venture and continue without falling to the end. Let us be careful that we do not go against temptation in our own strength. None of us is sufficient of himself, but our sufficiency is of God. The throne of grace has no lock on it, and is always open to the sinner who flees to it, to Him who sits on it without a frown or any displeasure toward any sinner who comes to Him. There is a welcome at court to the returning sinner, whatever he has been, and the way has been opened through blood, and the veil torn from top to bottom. Now the way is open to the Father for the weakest, poorest, most miserable person alive. There is a welcome in the face of the greatest sickness and poverty of every sort, and righteousness available to those who have nothing with which to pay. Blessed be God for freedom to the throne of grace!

If you want to bear fruit, go often to the throne of grace, for the people who are most fruitful are those who are most frequent at the throne. Those who are most poor in spirit, those who are most frequently on their knees, those who make most use of His name to approach the Father by Him, and who seek Him most often in earnest petitions—they are the ones who are most fruitful and whose ways please God. To go to the throne is beneficial for producing fruit, and bearing fruit is a help to go to the throne. Going to the throne is everything in the matter of producing fruit; and bearing fruit is an aid to go to the throne. It is from the throne that we are enabled to keep the commandments, that is, by the grace of the Father, in the name of the Son, and through the help of the Holy Spirit. And although it is from the throne that we have strength to keep the commandments, yet the apostle John says that we receive because we keep His commandments. There is a marvelous paradox here. "And whatsoever we ask, we receive of him, because we keep his commandments, and do those things that are pleasing in his sight" (1 John 3:22). A life contrary to the law casts a cloud between us and the throne, hinders prayer, and confuses the soul. There is strength at the throne to keep the commandments, and keeping them is an encouragement to go again to the throne. There is a remarkable concord in the plan. We go to the throne in order to bear fruit, and by bearing fruit we have clear access to the throne. For this reason, be often at the throne so that you bear much fruit. Let me say some things finally by way of applying this truth, and pray that the Lord will apply it.

First, we must ask the question of self-examination. We ask seriously on behalf of God: have you chosen Christ? Have you received Him as Savior, as King, and as everything to you? How can you know? Christ is more than everyone and than everything to the soul that chooses Him. If you haven't done so, or if this language sounds foreign to you, then you have not chosen Him yet. Well, you may say, "If I am still without Him, what shall I do?" Cry from the depth of your soul. Ask the Father in His name for a heart to choose. Ask for reality, life, salvation; for an ark before the flood, and a shelter from the fire that cannot be extinguished, for that which will make you happy to eternity.

Second, you who have chosen Him, give Him the praise, and thank Him for first choosing you and taking hold of you until you came to choose Him. Thank Him for the fact that Jesus chooses the weak, poor, feeble, and helpless, because this is how He found you. Therefore let none be disheartened. Here you have every welcome and strong encouragement. Oh, dear friends, come to the throne with all your burdens, needs, and wants of whatever kind, and whatever your character, weak, helpless, timid, fearful, afflicted, trembling, troubled. Come, sinners of every sort, that all your needs may be supplied from the inexhaustible treasury of grace. Let the poor come to be strengthened, the helpless to be confirmed, the afflicted to be comforted, the fearful to be assured, and the failing to be aided. Our weakness is no obstacle to our being saved. Rather, it is when we see only destruction awaiting us that there is greatest hope for us. If we will be saved, it is His work, and the renown will be His alone and for ever.

Oh, infinite God! We are astonished that Thou hast directed Thine eyes to look upon people like us. It is a wonder that Thou hast even noticed us except with a frown, and that Thou hast looked on us at all except to judge us and to summon us to appear at the judgment. And how amazing that Thou wouldst have anything to do with us apart from condemning us! Keep us with our eyes looking upward, and our hands stretched forth to heaven, our souls rejoicing, praising, and worshipping Him who loved us and first chose us. We have nothing of ourselves but our sins. The only thing we ever had was poverty, but Thou hast passed by us when we were polluted in our own blood, and Thou hast raised us from the great deep. Do it again with many more, and call, turn, move, save, and raise many more from their carelessness. Stir them from their spiritual sleep, and awaken them from their great apathy. Show them their danger and their peril while they may be saved. Convince them of the evil of their condition, while they may recover. Amen.

The Saints Loving Christ and Delighting in Him

"Whom having not seen, ye love; in whom, though now ye see him not, yet believing, ye rejoice with joy unspeakable and full of glory."
—1 Peter 1:8

Most people love objects that are visible; they delight in things that are seen. This is not to say that it is unworthy of men to love things or to take delight in objects, but there is a great debate among mankind as to things which are worth loving, and things in which we ought to take pleasure. There are two opinions, and those who hold them have been locked in debate since the beginning of the world; furthermore, there is no sign of the argument abating while both parties remain. One maintains that it is the invisible that we ought to love, and in which we should delight, while the other regards as strange those who love what is not seen, and thinks it is foolishness to find pleasure in such things, insisting that it is the visible that should be loved and in which happiness is to be found. For my part (and I cannot do less than assert to which party I belong), I am of the opinion that there is not one visible object worth loving very much, and in which very much pleasure is to be sought.

Many think that only visible things are substantial, and that those which are invisible belong to the imagination. We believe, however, that it is the invisible which has any substance and that it is the visible that is imaginary. To support us in this opinion, we have the wisest man who ever lived: Solomon says concerning things that are seen, "Vanity of vanities, saith the Preacher, vanity of vanities; all is vanity" (Eccl. 1:2). Look at anything you like, if you can see it, it is vanity; the invisible is real, the visible is imaginary. Objects that are seen last only for a time, but those that are not seen last forever. And since it is only the invisible that have any substance, they are the things we ought to love, and they alone are the things in which we should delight.

When we rejoice in the things that are not seen, many people in the world regard us as enthusiasts, saying that all we have is imagination. We respond that they love things that are insignificant and are taken up with the poorest things that exist. They are like people who play cards. There they are with their pieces of paper with marks on them to be turned and placed, one like this, another like that. This they call happiness because the objects are visible. Although they are nothing but pieces of paper they think that is enough to clear them of the charge of enthusiasm. Others are very active in what they call hunting—looking at one irrational creature running after another, and regarding that as cause for delight and pleasure. In the face of this we maintain that it is the invisible things which possess substance, and these are the objects which are worthy and deserving of our rejoicing and which infinitely merit our love.

The apostle was writing to those strangers scattered across the various countries named, and who were chosen by God to be sanctified by the Spirit, to have a part in the obedience of Jesus Christ, to receive an invisible inheritance, to be purified through trials, to be perfected through tribulations, and at last made fit for eternal glory. Speaking of the way in which their faith was being tested through various trials, he says that they would receive the end of their faith, the salvation of their souls. Then comes the text: "Whom (that is Christ) having not seen, ye love; in whom, though now ye see him not, yet believing, ye rejoice with joy unspeakable and full of glory." The apostle was telling these people two things about themselves, one negative and the other positive. The negative was that they had not seen Christ. Christ was seen in their lifetime; they could have seen Him with their own eyes, but they did not live where Christ walked the earth when He was in the form of a servant. And they could not see Him when the apostle was writing, for He had disappeared from sight, invisible to human eyes, to sit at the right hand of the Father. He will not be seen again until He comes on the clouds of heaven. This is implied in the words that He will come again visibly—"though now ye see him not"—as if to say, "You will see Him." Eyes would be given to the dust of the grave to see the Redeemer alive. "For I know that my redeemer liveth, and that he shall stand at the latter day upon the earth: and though after my skin worms destroy this body, yet in my flesh shall I see God: whom I shall see for myself, and mine eyes shall behold, and not another; though my reins be consumed within me" (Job 19:25-27). They had not seen Him when He was to be seen, and now He was not to be seen.

The positive thing he said to the people was that they believed. Believing corresponds to seeing. Believing is related to the soul as seeing is to the body. There is no such thing as believing in what is seen: believing is instead of seeing. Furthermore, believing is as effective as seeing. To believe that God is in this place is the same to us as to see Him, and has the same effect on us. If God is in this place and I believe that He is here, it has the same effect on me as if I saw God. A man who does not recognize the presence of God is like a child playing, hiding his face and saying, "You can't see me now." Believing that Christ will come on the clouds of heaven has the same effect on a man as if he actually saw Him coming on the clouds. Believing according to the measure of faith has the same effect as seeing, and if it is not so with you, you do not believe. If these effects do not accompany your believing, it is not true faith.

The apostle speaks here to these people about loving Christ and rejoicing in Him, and that with a joy that is strong, heavenly, spiritual, unspeakable, and glorious. I do not want to make any more comments on believing, but I want to draw attention to two other matters, namely, loving Christ and rejoicing in Christ. Since believing they loved, and since believing and loving they were rejoicing.

Let us consider these thoughts:

    I. Every godly man on earth loves Christ
    II. Every godly man rejoices in Christ

I. Every godly man on earth loves Christ
    If anyone leaves the world without loving Christ, he will not

be saved. "If any man love not the Lord Jesus Christ, let him be anathema," hateful and accursed until the coming of the Lord (1 Cor. 16:22). Everyone who does not love the Lord Jesus Christ is ungodly, cursed, out of favor with God, liable to the wrath of God, without hope and without God in the world. He is unacceptable to and rejected by God.

Every man loves something; man is a creature that loves something. He has the ability and the faculty to love. It is in his nature; loving something is as natural to him as seeing, moving, and breathing. Love is as essential to a human being as hands and feet. One of the faculties of his soul has been purposely fashioned to love. Nevertheless, man fell into such a condition through sin that he does not love, but rather hates Christ and God. But the inclination and nature that God in His infinite grace gives to those whom He saves brings them to love Christ. No one by nature loves Christ; yet Christ is infinitely worthy of being loved by all His creatures. He is worthy of being loved by virtue of His person, His offices, His work, His riches, and His abundance. He is an object infinitely worthy of being loved.

Let me say a few words about love by way of description. The objects of love are these three: beauty, pleasantness, and goodness, either imaginary or real. It is the imaginary sort that many possess without the actual. It is all in the imagination. This is how it is with all who love sin. There is nothing pleasant or beautiful about sin, nor anything good, but they are found completely in Christ, perfectly and really. There is nothing in Christ except beauty, comeliness, and goodness. In His person, His offices, His work, and His properties He is infinitely lovely, pleasant, and good. In order that we may know to whom and about whom of my listeners we can say, "Whom, having not seen, ye love," here are some of the features of those who love Christ (1 Pet. 1:8). I know I can say these words to some, but I do not know whether I can say them to everyone or not. If, instead of speaking generally, I could speak to everyone here individually, and ask, "Do you love the Lord Jesus Christ," I wonder how many could answer according to the words of the text. Now, however, I want everyone to examine himself in particular while I speak to the congregation in general.

1. Those who love Christ love Him first, chiefly, and above all else. There is no such thing as loving Christ less than other things or people. If you think that you love Christ, and love other things before Him, you are mistaken. Whoever loves Christ leaves everything for His sake. If you love Christ, you hate the best that earth has to offer when they come between you and Him. If you love Christ, your love for relatives, parents, children, brothers and sisters, possessions and life is but hatred in comparison. Be honest with yourselves, because what will it profit you in the judgment to have some fancy or imagination instead of the truth? If you do not love Christ above all else, you do not love Him at all.

2. If you love Christ, you entrust your cause to Him. If you love Christ you will not be stubborn, saying, "He does not want me," or "He will not receive me." Many give a false name to this kind of attitude, calling it great humility. Far from it; such thoughts betray narrow ideas of Christ and unworthy conceptions of God. If you love Christ, that will help you to entrust the cause of your soul to Him. He is able to keep what you have committed to Him "against that day." If you love Christ, you gave what you have to Him to keep. This meeting will be one entirely given to self-examination.

3. If you love Christ, you will love the means of communion with Christ; you will be often in those places where you will meet Him, that is, before the throne of grace, reading the Bible, and concerning yourself with the ordinances of the gospel, the very places where the King walks. Is it so with you, dear soul?

4. Those who love Christ love the image of Christ on earth. They love those best in whom the likeness of Christ is most clearly seen. We ought to love every man because he is a man, but we ought to love him more because he has the image of Christ on him. We ought to love the Turks, Chinese, Kaffirs, and all the pagans of earth because they are men. Indeed, we ought to love our enemies, those who fight against us, as men, but we ought to love those who

love Christ because of His image. We ought to love most those who have the image of Christ, and love most especially those who have most of His image. Those who love Christ love His image.

5. Those who love Christ are distressed, uneasy, and anxious when He hides Himself. There is sorrow and confusion when He hides His face. "Thou didst hide thy face, and I was troubled" (Ps. 30:7). It does not matter to some what kind of service they have, nor what kind of prayer in the family—as long as they receive good gifts they are satisfied, without knowing about Christ smiling or hiding Himself. But the man who loves Christ is in great distress when Christ is out of his sight. He goes home from the service sometimes with such a heavy heart that others are amazed at him. "Why are you so sad today? Were you in the service?" "Yes." "Was there a preacher?" "Yes." "Did he have many gifts?" "He had the best gifts." "Was his sermon short?" "Oh no! He preached for nearly an hour." "Well, why are you so sad after the service?" "Because I did not see the face of Christ there."

6. Whoever loves Christ is very careful to keep the commandments of Christ. "If ye love me, keep my commandments." Antinomians talk much about loving Christ, but their lives declare that they do not love Him, because they do not keep His commandments. Those who love Christ strive to their utmost to keep all the commands of the moral law.

7. Whoever loves Christ loves to do something for Christ. They are not concerned so much with what they do as that they have something to do. There are many who want some great and noble work, but these want only to do something for Christ. The godly Newton of London speaks of two angels. He says, "If the Lord sent two angels and set one of them to rule an empire and the other to sweep the street, the one who swept the street would be as delighted with his office as the other on the throne. In the same way the godly man is as happy in his position, even if it is only teaching a child, as is the greatest preacher. He is as zealous in his work, because it is for his Lord."

8. The man who loves Christ is content to suffer for Christ. It is true that there is not much suffering for religion today, especially in Britain, apart from suffering an occasional blasphemy and a little mockery. Such suffering is not worth mentioning. Yet it is too much for some to undergo. Perhaps if they are called names by someone they set the law on him, but the godly man is prepared to suffer for Christ if need be. Every godly man is just as ready now to go home through the fire for the sake of Christ as the godly martyrs of a previous age. It is true that there is not the power now as they had because there is not the need. But if the situation arose, the strength would be given. The godly is pleased, if need be, to be counted worthy to suffer for the sake of the Son of man.

9. The godly man thirsts to see Christ as He is, and to go home to live with Him. I will not say much about this, since my conscience pricks me when I preach beyond my experience. I cannot say I am wholly ignorant of this experience, yet it is too rare. But this is true of godliness, there is a "looking for that blessed hope, and the glorious appearing of the great God and our Saviour Jesus Christ" (Titus 2:13). It is sad to think of those who are here who do not love Christ. I can say as Peter said to Simon, "I perceive that thou art in the gall of bitterness, and in the bond of iniquity" (Acts 8:23). Although you have a great name, it is nothing but vanity, and if you are not brought to love Christ you are one of the offenders who will be cast out of the kingdom of Christ.

II. Every godly man rejoices in Christ

"I do not think," says someone, "that there is any joy in religion." Well, friend, I respond that I do not think that there is any joy in anything except religion. Some say that religion is nothing but a cause of melancholy and sadness. It is surely surprising if religion, which is of God, a sea of happiness, makes men melancholy. That which came from the unfailing fountain of pleasure, nurturing sadness! Religion, which came from God in whose presence there is always a fullness of joy, bearing no fruit but melancholy or depression! "Well, they are the ones we seem to be most sad, and if there is joy in religion, why are those who are religious so sad and mournful?" I will tell you. It is either hypocrisy or opposition to their religion that continually makes them sad. It is like the noise of the wind, for example. The noise it makes is not so much in itself as in the houses and trees which restrict its movement. They cause the sound. The wind goes on its way swiftly and noiselessly, but it meets many obstacles which cause the frightening tumult and disturbance which are sometimes heard. It is the same with the sound of the river. The noise is not in the rivers or the waters, but in the hindrances they encounter. If there were no rocks and uneven places which so often stand in their way, the rivers would glide by as slowly and quietly as the Ganges in India, the Nile in Egypt, or the Severn and Mersey in Britain. If it were not for these, the rivers would be as calm as they are all over the face of the earth. It is exactly the same with the Christian—it is the plague of the heart, the corruption of the breast, enmity to God, the body of death and all the obstacles to religion that occasion mourning in religion. But joy in Christ is essential to true religion. God, grant an awakening in the conscience of every man to consider the matter for himself. The conscience of many a person here tells him that he has never rejoiced in Christ, and yet he vainly hopes that he is godly. I do not say that godly men know nothing of occasions and periods, but it is certain that to some degree this joy in Christ Jesus is found in every godly man.

Joy in Christ is in the nature of religion. "For we are the circumcision, which worship God in the spirit, and rejoice in Christ Jesus, and have no confidence in the flesh" (Phil. 3:3). Those who did, or sometimes do rejoice? No, we are those who *are* such. What about them? We are the circumcision. You and others like you? No, we alone. Those who rejoice in Christ Jesus are the only godly ones on the earth, and the only true Israelites in the world. Not only the Methodists, but some from the Church of England, some from the Independents, and from every name and party who are of this description, they believe in the Lord Jesus and rejoice in Him. And are there no godly apart from these? No, there is not one, from any nation or country or any part of the world. Who are they? "We are the circumcision." Who are you? Those who "rejoice in Christ Jesus." "For the kingdom of God is not meat and drink; but righteousness, and peace, and joy in the Holy Ghost." "I perceive that thou art in the gall of bitterness, and in the bond of iniquity." "The fruit of the Spirit is...joy" (Gal. 5:22). "And again I say, Rejoice" (Phil. 4:4). The man who does not rejoice in Christ is not godly—this much is sure and obvious.

Christ is so infinitely lovely that it is impossible to know Him without loving Him, and to believe in Him without rejoicing in Him; and love to Christ is such that it is impossible to love Him without rejoicing in Him. What is joy? I could give you a philosophical description. Joy is the delight the mind takes in an object on account of its attractiveness, its beauty, and its goodness; or in other words, the mind taking pleasure in the sight of something attractive, beautiful, or good; or in the possession of something attractive, beautiful, and good; or in the strong hope of enjoying it. I think this description would satisfy any philosopher present.

There are many kinds of joy:
1. There is a natural joy. This joy is positive, harmless in itself.
2. There is an unnatural joy. This can be seen in the case of someone in distress or trouble or great anxiety delighting in or wishing for the grave, like Job or Jeremiah.
3. There is a diabolical, devilish, hellish joy. Joy in sin does not deserve a better name.
4. There is a spiritual joy. This is the joy referred to in the text.

I wish to say two things about spiritual joy: one concerns temporal spiritual joy, and the other eternal spiritual joy. Temporal joy is illustrated in the seed which fell on stony ground, appearing for a time and then vanishing. There are many like this who have tasted of the heavenly gift and the powers of the world to come, and yet have fallen away. Their joy dies and their candle is extinguished in the utter darkness. However, others have eternal spiritual joy which lasts forever, and this is the joy possessed by every one who loves Christ.

Again, I observe the following about joy in Christ:

1. It is in the means of grace that joy in Christ is to be found, not in dreams, imaginations, or visions. Nor is it to be found in fancying that you hear a voice from heaven and thinking that you are godly and the like. It is not through things like this that joy in Christ is to be obtained, but by the means of grace. "Therefore with joy shall ye draw water out of the wells of salvation" (Isa. 12:3).

2. This joy in Christ always comes after some trial or distress or great trouble. It comes to him who has been pricked in his heart, brought to stand under Sinai, been shaken over hell, made to see his lost condition, whose hope in the law has been utterly destroyed until he has been driven to cry, "What must I do to be saved?" and who receives in time a sight of Christ. The man brought by God to trouble, distress, intense hardship, mourning, anxiety, pain, and death, and in this circumstance is shown the salvation of God—this is the man who rejoices in Christ. "A woman when she is in travail hath sorrow, because her hour is come: but as soon as she is delivered of the child, she remembereth no more the anguish, for joy that a man is born into the world" (John 16:21). The person who has this joy has been in pain and distress like a woman in labor. How many of you have been pricked in your hearts, know about the distress of this condition, have been convicted of sin, and can say "sin revived, and I died," have experienced the cares of death, and instead of seeking life through the law have died to it? Have you been in anguish, distress, and tribulation until you have been forced to cry out, "What shall I do?" Have you in that distress received a sight of the Savior, and salvation, perfect, prepared, full, free, meeting your very need? The man who rejoices in Christ is just such a man. Search the Scriptures to see whether these things are so.

3. Joy in Christ brings a man down to the dust. The man who rejoices in Christ is the lowliest and poorest man there is. We would not be proud or difficult to handle if we rejoiced in Christ. The

effect of this joy is humility and self-loathing. "And I will establish my covenant with thee; and thou shalt know that I am the LORD: that thou mayest remember, and be confounded" (Ez. 16:62-63). I will make peace with you, my indignation against you will be removed, I will be appeased. What effects does this peace have upon the man? It causes him to blush, to be ashamed, to hide his face, to fear to show his face because of his disgrace.

4. Joy in Christ is like oil on wheels: it facilitates the walk, renews strength, and provides means to run without tiring or fainting. This is what causes you to say, "His commandments are not grievous" (1 John 5:3). The yoke of His commands is easy and His burden light. This joy enables some to run without being weary, to travel without tiring, and takes them on without their knowing, swiftly like the chariots of Aminadab.

5. Joy in Christ conquers earthly joy. It is in vain that fleshly joy is offered to the man who has this joy. It is foolish to expect the son of a prince or a king to exchange his amusements with the children of the street, and to leave the playthings fitting for him in his exalted state and to play with the poor children of the town. It is foolish to bring the empty pleasures of the earth to a man whose heart is full of the joy of Christ. It overcomes the joy of earth, yes, and the sadness of this world as well.

6. Joy in Christ intoxicates a man until he forgets his care. Possessed of this joy, he can be happy when there is no fruit in the fields, when the olive and the vine have no yield, when nature fails, the earth frowns, and earthly objects retreat, when he is in the valley of the shadow of death. This joy will be at its strongest when the joy of earth will have perished.

What kind of joy is the joy that is in Christ? Let me say three things about it. It is great joy; it is joy unspeakable; it is glorious joy. In the first place, it is a great joy. "Ye greatly rejoice." The joy of the world is short, empty, and weak; but the joy in Christ is continuous, great, and strong. It is joy in a great object; it comes from a great fountain; and it will result in a great heaven presently.

Secondly, it is joy unspeakable, a joy beyond the power of speech to express or of tongue to proclaim. Is it any wonder that those who have this joy should make such unusual gestures while they are rejoicing? They cannot express themselves in words; they do not have the ability or the gifts. There is more in them than they can bring out. Theirs is joy *unspeakable*. These people are like the liquid in the bottle that bubbles when it is poured out because the neck of the bottle is too narrow. The bottle is fuller than the neck can cope with; the soul is fuller than the tongue can cope with. Do you wonder at us rejoicing, and the strange appearance some have when they rejoice? It is because we cannot express ourselves. If we could say what we wanted to, we would do so as we sat. If we had enough gifts to relate our joy, we would give an account with our arms folded—but the joy is unspeakable!

Furthermore, the joy is glorious: joy in a glorious object, joy in a glorious person, and the beginning of a glorious work. There is joy in a glorious object. Jesus is the object, and He is an infinitely glorious object. We have seen many rejoicing and exulting, and after that, they are a sorry spectacle. Yes, indeed, but this is not so with joy in Christ. The godly experience sorry circumstances, but no one who rejoices in Christ becomes ungodly. This is joy with sufficiency behind it, and so it will always be. Furthermore, there is joy in a glorious person. This is joy in the Holy Ghost. The Spirit is its author. It is not our temperament or faculties that produce it but the gifts of the Spirit. The Spirit acts on our faculties. It is He who plays like a musician on his harp, and sometimes inflames them with joy out of love for the Savior of sinners. Finally, this joy is the beginning of a glorious work. The meetings will end, both special and public; and preaching and praying will soon end forever. But joy in Christ will never end. This will last forever and ever. This is a work, begun on earth, which will last after the world is burned. After every other joy has perished, this joy will be at its most powerful and will continue so. The joy of the believer in Christ is a great, unspeakable, glorious joy.

Who has experienced this joy? Who are those who possess this great, unspeakable, and glorious joy in Christ? Someone says, "I did have it. I experienced it a long time ago, but I do not have it today—I know nothing about it now." Why are you like this? Do you not know? If I asked a widow, "Why are you so sad?" she would answer directly that it was because her husband was dead. If I asked someone else, "Why do you look so miserable? How did you lose your joy?" he would say, "My house caught fire and I have lost everything." But Zion, is your husband dead? Have your possessions caught fire? Has the bank of the covenant broken? Is not Jesus alive? Has His grace failed? What is the reason and cause that your joy and delight are no longer what they were? Is not the salvation of God as glorious, and His gracious words as pleasing as ever they were? "Awake, awake; put on thy strength, O Zion.... Shake thyself from the dust; arise and sit down, O Jerusalem: loose thyself from the bands of thy neck" (Isa. 52:1-2). Take your harp down from the willow from shame. Jesus is altogether the same. Christ is the same and His grace as complete as ever, His relationship with you is the same, and the covenant also is the same. Why, therefore, has your joy vanished and your delight grown less?

Ah! I know what it is. You have offended the Beloved, you have grieved the Comforter; you went to play with some objects that were not lawful. You caused the heaviness and mourning that you feel presently with your sins. Therefore, humble yourself, fall down, fall at His feet, and cry, "Forgive me, wash me, take away from me the things that cause Thee to turn Thy face away, and let me see Thy face again that I may rejoice again."

Who would not rejoice at the rescue of his life from destruction, at being set free from extreme distress, at having his life hidden, and being liberated from prison? If you knew it, if you experienced these things, you would rejoice in them. Christ is an object of joy to all who know Him. May we all be made partakers of this joy, and possessors of it. Amen.

Printed in the United Kingdom by
Lightning Source UK Ltd., Milton Keynes
137102UK00001B/189/A